FROM
THESE ROOTS

FROM THESE ROOTS

BRINGING LIGHT, HOPE, AND TRANSFORMATION TO ATLANTA'S INNER CITY

A Journey of Two Brothers

....

JEFF DEEL

MAXWELL
LEADERSHIP.

Published by Maxwell Leadership Publishing, an imprint of Forefront Books, Nashville, Tennessee.

Distributed by Simon & Schuster.

Library of Congress Control Number: 2023920031

Print ISBN: 979-8-88710-272-6
E-book ISBN: 979-8-88710-273-3

Cover Design by Bruce Gore, Gore Studio, Inc.
Interior Design by Mary Susan Oleson, Blu Design Concepts

Printed in the United States of America

THIS BOOK IS DEDICATED TO
Cecil and Dawn Deel.
It is their investment in their children
that has produced the eternal return
you will read about on these pages.

Contents

Foreword
By Keith Deel

ONLY THIRTEEN MONTHS separate the birthdays of Bruce and Jeff Deel, and since their arrival on this planet, that thirteen months is about the only time they have not been together in some way. Born as children of an itinerant Pentecostal preacher from the coal mining town of War, West Virginia, and his young wife from the rustic riverbank settlement of Allisonia, Virginia, Bruce and Jeff had humble beginnings to say the least. It was from the small and budding churches where their father evangelized and pastored that the two would learn to work together to have a positive impact on the lives of thousands of others growing up in poverty and experiencing life's deepest struggles of addiction, abuse, abandonment, and other aleatory situations.

Bruce, being the firstborn, took on the role of leader and protector early in life. Jeff, on the other hand, was gifted as an organizer, planner, and analytical thinker. He also had the gift of picking on me, and since I was family, I think Bruce just saw this as free entertainment since we did not have a lot of toys while growing up. I was used as the middleman during their wrestling escapades; I was dropped over and over from the hayloft of an old barn on the farm where we once lived; I was baptized to the point of nearly drowning; I was used as a punching bag; and finally, one dark night, I was bound hand and foot and left for dead in a graveyard. Growing up as the younger brother of these two was not always a comfortable position to be in.

Through these tough times, I saw Bruce and Jeff's personality differences very early in life, but little did I know that those differences would later complement one another as they worked as a team to create scenarios of opportunity, bringing comfort to those hurting, broken, and lost.

During their young lives, Bruce and Jeff were inseparable, if for no other *reason* than Jeff often found himself in need of someone to protect him, and to finish the battles he somehow won mentally but needed help closing out physically. On more than one occasion, Jeff would find himself on the wrong end of an altercation, looking for someone to come to the rescue. Thus, Bruce learned early on that one of his main roles in life was to protect, defend, and fight for those who were in some type of trouble. Bruce was born with an innate desire and ability to jump in the middle of a problem, and if that problem continued or grew, he would then almost supernaturally exert a physical presence that would end with the other party surrendering and just walking away, or receiving a beatdown that they had not seen coming from a skinny, wiry, red-headed country boy.

I don't know if Bruce ever lost a fight, but if he did, the other guy or guys felt like they lost as well. Unfortunately for others, Jeff learned that Bruce would not walk away from trouble, but would always engage, and so he began to pick fights and cause trouble just so he could watch Bruce take care of the issue that had been created. He may have developed this sinister behavior so Bruce's energy would be spent on some unsuspecting victim instead of on Jeff himself. Over time, I can imagine Jeff sought out problems just to see how his older brother would solve them, started fights just to see his brother finish them, and took risks knowing that his near twin would save the day.

I remember sitting with Jeff at a Church of God district rally service at the Charlottesville Southside Church of God in 1978. I don't remember any of the songs that were sung that night. I don't remember who preached or what they preached about. However, I do remember getting pinched by my mother, which was a form of discipline supposed to make me sit still, but actually had the exact opposite effect! The greatest memory from that night was Bruce spending what seemed like an exorbitant amount of time at the altar at the front of the church, with lots of people laying their hands on him and praying. I remember him standing up and there being quite a commotion and even making declarations about God working in his life. From that night forward, there were conversations and comments made about Bruce being called to preach, and I found that pretty interesting as

11

a twelve-year-old boy who was still trying to find reasons to be in church. However, I recall feeling there was something different about that night. An excitement, joy, lots of tears, and I guess you could say a pinch from the Holy Spirit. A pinch on a young man's life, which also caused him to not be still.

Bruce had never been still. He had a way of constantly moving forward into the next activity, game, or fight. But now, he had received a pinch of direction, of correction, of favor. He would now walk; no, he would now run the path before him, run the race of his calling, and he would run to win the prize. Never doubting from that night in 1978 the prize was to help, encourage, fight for, and even carry those who didn't know they could run. Little did Bruce know that joining the race beside him and his future wife, Rhonda, would be his closest friend, a twin of favor, who would be closer than a brother. It is from this "side by side" perspective that Jeff Deel can best tell the story of the work God has done and is doing through the combined personalities, differences, and gifts of he and his brother, Bruce.

Bruce and Jeff's journey out of the pristine rural mountainous regions of Virginia started not far from the humble beginnings of such visionaries as Patrick Henry, Thomas Jefferson, and Booker T. Washington. From there, God placed Bruce and Jeff and their families on a new pathway and led them to those with deep needs and no hope in some of the most destitute neighborhoods in America and

Jamaica. Through their obedience to God's purpose, Bruce and Jeff have called the hopeless to transformative action, instructed and educated survivors and those who have experienced unimaginable pain and grief, and ultimately, they have witnessed God's sons and daughters being set free from physical and spiritual bondage. As Jeff shares their amazing and inspiring story in this book, I hope you join me and countless others in celebrating these runners in their "well done and faithful" race for the prize. After more than twenty-five years of leading with Light, offering Hope, and witnessing the Transformation of thousands around them, it seems they are just getting started.

Introduction

....

THIS BOOK IS about my brother Bruce and me. It is about
our roots, the important things that shaped us to become
the men we are today, and our faith. It is a book about the
discovery of our natural tendencies and bents, how we became
comfortable in our respective skins, and how we have lived
and worked from that comfortable place for many years. It is
about leadership and followership and how effort and impact
can be maximized when leaders lead well and followers loyally
follow without always assuming they are in training to be
leaders. Our lives prove that sometimes, if not all the time, it
is quite alright for followers to simply follow.

The first half of the book is composed of personal stories
about our lives as sons of a holiness preacher, who ambled
out of the hills and hollows of southern West Virginia in
1958 and found our mother waiting for him on the banks
of New River in a quaint village called Allisonia. The stories
are about adventure, pain, fire, love, fighting, loss, service,
benevolence, and calling. They are stories that exemplify the

human experience in general, but that are unique to our own humanity. We look back through the details of these stories and now understand we were being prepared for the work that is described in the second half of the book.

The stories in part 2 are born out of the work Bruce and I have done together at City of Refuge in the inner-city of Atlanta for the last quarter of a century. This is the work for which we were being prepared. Bruce founded the ministry in 1997, and I joined him in 1998. Together we have labored to bring Light, Hope, and Transformation to children in crisis situations, homeless citizens, people who have been victimized by opportunity injustice, survivors of sex trafficking and exploitation, and addicts looking for a pathway to freedom.

To be clear, neither Bruce, nor I, nor the strong team we have built at City of Refuge, are the heroes. We are merely the guides. Those who have overcome tremendous obstacles to not only survive but thrive are the heroes. It has been our honor to serve them through the years, and it is an honor to tell their stories now.

In some cases, names have been changed and generalizations have been made for the purpose of ensuring that the telling of their stories does not become a form of exploitation, or to keep a layer of protection around those we serve from bad people who may still want to do them harm. It is my goal that our friends who have landed on the pages of this book will read it and feel dignified and respected. It is also my goal that you, the reader, will read to the last page, place the book on a shelf in your home or office, or better yet, pass it on to a friend or relative for them to read, and walk away with a great sense of satisfaction in knowing that doing bad things is not necessarily an indication that the doer is a bad person, and that opportunity is a great savior.

When contemplating how to best introduce you to the vastly different persons of Bruce and Jeff Deel, and how our relationship works, my mind went to a spring day in 1996, two years before I started to work with Bruce in Atlanta. I was sitting on the veranda at my home in Jamaica, admiring the clever work I had done on the clothesline in the yard below. A few weeks earlier, my wife, Tracy, and I had packed up a few belongings, and with our four children in tow, had moved to the island to work at a vocational training center for young men who had been unable to succeed in traditional education pathways. Compared to our comfortable lifestyle in a two-story, four-bedroom house on a tree-lined cul-de-sac in Atlanta, life in Jamaica was relatively primitive. Neither our dwelling nor our vehicle had air-conditioning, and Jamaica is every bit as hot as Georgia. Entertainment consisted of watching crusty beetles dive-bomb into our Kool-Aid, and weekly trips to the beach replaced TV and movies, which wasn't so bad.

Additionally, we had left behind perfectly good Maytag laundry appliances and now turned our soiled garments over to a domestic helper, who would take turns dipping them into a bucket of soapy water and scrubbing them alternately against themselves and against a rock. After rinsing, the clothes were hung on the clothesline to dry, a practice my grandparents and even my mother, during my early years, had exercised, but that I was just fine living without.

Watching T-shirts and Fruit of the Looms flutter in the island breeze was romantic until they became low-hanging fruit for a kid goat that lived on the property. Sammy, the name my kids attached to the cute little gray and white creature, had been purchased by a young man on our staff to raise for his wedding reception, which was a year away. It was intended that, aside from the bride and groom, Sammy would be the star of the show at the reception, but I will forego the details. Let's just say, *All give some, and some give all.* Sammy falls in the latter category.

As if he knew the fate that had been decided for him, Sammy spent his days looking for ways to create fun and folly at the expense of the humans who were planning his demise. He scattered garbage all over the property, destroyed freshly manicured flower gardens, and pulled newly washed garments from the clothesline, dragging them through the yard with all the goat-pride he could muster. It was infuriating.

On this particular island morning, I made no effort to squelch my own pride as I watched little Sammy prance into the yard from around the corner of the building. He came with his usual cocky gait, chin held high and the hint of a smile on his face. He was about to bring ruination to a week's worth of clean duds, or so he thought, and he was relishing the moment.

To the surprise of the little mischief maker, he couldn't reach the clothes. The long sticks I had notched and used to prop up the line made me the victor, finally. Or so *I* thought.

As I leaned back in my chair and began to hum "We Are the Champions," I saw Leon come into the yard as well. Leon was a horse we had taken from a thoroughbred breeder a few days earlier when we found out they planned to euthanize him. He had been oddly situated inside his mother, causing a traumatic birth that ended in her death, and leaving him with a head shaped like a lima bean. According to his owner, "It wouldn't matter if he was faster than Secretariat, you can't take him to the track with a head like that. It would not be proper." And Jamaicans are nothing if not proper.

What happened next is hardly believable, but it's true. Sammy began to run circles around the yard and jump wildly toward the hanging laundry, but his vertical leap was lacking. He was on a mission but could not produce the desired results without help. Calmly, Leon approached the line, tilted his head upward, and began to nibble at a clothespin until it popped loose. The shirt dropped down on one side, making it easily accessible to the goat, who promptly grabbed it and took off like he was being chased by a cheetah. By the time I reached the yard, Leon had disengaged three more clothespins, but I rescued the remaining laundry before the goat returned.

Sammy went on to serve his purpose among the people and became an inextricable part of their lives. When my family returned to America, Leon went back to the horse farm under the agreement that he would not be discarded just because he was ugly. He spent his days grazing in lush pastures, away from the stares of curious human onlookers but perfectly comfortable in the company of other thorough-breds who seemed not to care about his crooked head.

I told the story of the goat, the horse, and the laundry to a wise, elderly Jamaican woman and asked if she had an interpretation of its meaning.

She thought for a moment and gave me an answer I have never forgotten. She said that the goat is a dreamer who has visions of big accomplishments, but who will not realize the fulfillment of his dreams alone and without help. The horse, though flawed and limited in his own ways, comes with abili-ties the goat does not have and is there to support the dream, though it is not his own. Both are limited by time and space and the agendas of other entities, but together they will accom-plish all that is possible in the time they have.

Okay, I admit she did not say it exactly like that, but it's a beefed-up paraphrase of her analysis.

Bruce and I came from humble beginnings, growing up in a part of the country where killing hogs and "putting up" preserves were annual traditions. Our father was a country preacher who met our mother at a little white church on a hillside near New River in southwest Virginia, married her five weeks later, and gave her the life she had prayed for. Together they had four children, Bruce, Jeff, Keith, and April, the oldest two being the subjects of this narrative.

Growing up in southwest and central Virginia, Bruce and I learned how to take on challenges, how to deal with adversity, and most of all, how to work as a team. It was apparent early on that Bruce was a leader and I was a follower. Our personalities and skill sets were, and still are, immensely different, and for many years we have used that to our advantage. He is Sammy, and I am Leon.

To illustrate, when Bruce was seventeen and I was sixteen, we were returning from a youth group outing in Charlottesville to our home in rural Albemarle County. It was late and we were trying to make curfew, which was commonplace for us. Bruce was behind the wheel of his 1973 Ford Pinto, which is one step up from a Hot Wheels car, and I was in the passenger seat. As was the case with most cars in those days, the Pinto only had lap belts, which no one used, so we would identify as a couple of pinballs if the little car were to go out of control or flip. He was negotiating the curves on the narrow road like he was driving the Grand Prix, which was also common. We rounded a particularly steep curve and instantly found ourselves in the middle of a herd of cattle that had escaped the confines of nearby fenced fields, and at fifty miles per hour, it seemed we were doomed to meet our Maker, riding into heaven, hopefully, on the back of a steer or heifer, as there was no clear pathway through the animals.

What followed is a blur, but the end result is very clear. Bruce never tapped the brake pedal; rather, he navigated his way through tens of thousands of pounds of beef still on the hoof, and we came out on the other side without so much as a bovine hair on the Pinto.

I'm sure I didn't understand it then, but in retrospect, the foreshadowing is palpable. Bruce has always been an adventurer, risk-taker, and innovator. Obstacles only seem to make the journey more fun, and very little thought is given to tapping the brakes when those obstacles appear, even if they come unannounced and out of nowhere, even if there are no plans or resources in place to address the problem. He is a realist who does not bury his head in the sand and act like the problem is not there, nor does he expect Providence to step in and fix everything just because he is a man of faith. But he is not going to slow down if he knows he is on the right road and the destination is true. He is on assignment, and the four pillars he has built his life and work on—Passion, Excellence, Dignity, and Integrity—are ever present as he exercises obedience to the assignment day by day.

Some people would have seen the cows as a challenge at best and a certain catastrophe at worst. I believe Bruce saw the situation as an opportunity to prove that the seemingly impossible could actually be achieved with big faith, a calm head, and a willingness to be adventurous and take risks. My reaction in the moment was to calmly point toward the herd and say, "Watch out for those cows."

For twenty-five years, Bruce and I have worked together at City of Refuge and have proven that teamwork between siblings is not only possible, but powerful productivity can be the result. In all that time, he has not slowed down in his pursuit of the dream and has remained steadfast in his commitment to his divine assignment. Every December he says, "Let's just get to the first of the year and things will slow down." And we laugh.

I have never really paused to write a description of my role at City of Refuge, but you might say I hung around to pop loose the clothespins or point out the cows in the road so he could run with his dreams. Our personality test results indicate that Bruce is an accelerator and I am glue. Seems like a good combination to move a vehicle toward its destination while holding things together in the process.

We exist to bring Light, Hope, and Transformation. This is the simple, eight-word mission statement of City of Refuge in Atlanta, Georgia. City of Refuge is the vehicle Bruce has driven for the past twenty-five years, a faith-based organization that has provided programs and services, such as housing, medical care, educational opportunities, vocational training, addiction recovery, and prisoner re-entry, to name a few, to tens of thousands of people, most of whom were up against seemingly immovable barriers to progress. And he has done it all under one roof in a beautiful and dynamic one-stop-shop on Atlanta's west side.

Picture a young mother with three children who has finally bailed out of a relationship with an abusive man, desperate enough to sneak out while he is away or asleep, desperate enough to leave without money because she has been totally dependent on him, desperate enough that she would rather her children huddle in the back seat of the car on cold winter nights than to have them tremble in the next room while *he* screams alcohol-induced profanities and slaps her around.

Picture a frantic and dirty teen girl who sprints onto your property, screaming that someone has to help her, screaming that "they" are after her and that "they" will kill her if they find her, begging for someone to take her to the courthouse so her name and social security number can be changed, begging for someone to help erase the fact that she ever existed.

Picture someone's beautiful daughter, who thinks she has finally discovered the love of her life, only to have him force her into the life of a sex slave, selling her first to family members, friends, and acquaintances, and eventually trafficking her across the country and abandoning her in Atlanta when she is arrested and goes to jail for the very thing he forced her to do. Picture this same girl being released from jail with nowhere to go and no one to call and ultimately claiming a cemetery as her home, her bed the ground behind some long-gone stranger's headstone.

Picture a little boy who leaves for school after a night of shouting, sirens, and gunshots, stepping over stoned relatives to get to the door of his apartment, and walking dirty streets to get to school, relying on free breakfast and lunch programs for his basic survival, and all day enduring the anxiety of having to go back home. At eight years of age, he has witnessed things no person of any age should have to witness—illicit drug use, sexual promiscuity, gang wars, and lifeless, bullet-riddled bodies lying on doorsteps and sidewalks in his own housing complex.

Picture a worn and weary man exiting the gates of the state prison after twenty-five years of being locked away from his family, friends, and all of society, a man who is wondering what's next and who is facing the same obstacles, influences, and challenges he faced before he was given a life sentence for being in the car with someone who killed a worker at a convenience store. Picture a convicted felon with little education, no job skills, no money or resources, and no healthy relationships.

The descriptions above are of actual people who have driven, ridden, walked, run, or crawled through the City of Refuge gates and have discovered their pathway to Transformation. And there are thousands more just like them. In the past quarter of a century, more than thirty thousand individuals have been introduced to the powerful process of Light, Hope, and Transformation. The goal is to break down barriers that hinder people from succeeding in life and to build momentum that leads to success.

Negative circumstances have a way of darkening the landscape, making it difficult to see a clear pathway forward. City of Refuge shines Light on the pathway by changing the circumstances. Homelessness becomes a warm, comfortable room that is beautifully decorated and exquisitely inviting.

25

Hunger becomes three nutritious meals per day in a clean dining hall with good company. Dragging young children around the city on public transportation while Mom tries to make appointments or job interviews becomes a safe, education-centered daycare environment only thirty steps from her room, freeing her up to do the things she needs to do.

Slowly the darkness begins to dissipate, and Light prevails. Unburdened from many of the circumstances that had dominated her previous life, she now has a clearer vision of the life that is possible.

But it is not good enough to simply remove obstacles with an expectation that people will know how to advance on their own. The next step is to set the stage for Hope to begin to grow like flowers in a well-watered, well-fertilized, and well-tended garden. An assessment of aptitude and skills creates a sense of confidence and capability, and eventual enrollment in a job training program, with all the supportive services in place, causes Hope to strengthen and flourish. We're on our way.

The end goal is Transformation. The barriers have been broken down and tremendous momentum is the result. Obedience to the process has resulted in a clear pathway to Transformation. Ultimately, the previously homeless mother drives her kids to school in her own dependable vehicle, heads to work at an IT company where she earns a salary of seventy thousand dollars annually, comes home in the evening and prepares a hot, nutritious meal, bathes the children in a clean tub, and tucks them into their own warm, comfortable beds.

The world Bruce and I grew up in was one of simplicity and wholesomeness. We spent our days in small rural schools, exploring fields and woods, riverbanks and railroad tracks, hollows and caves, and on sandlot football fields and dirt basketball courts. We rode steers and ponies, ran from bulls in the pasture, toyed with snakes we happened upon in our adventures, and jumped from the barn loft onto stacks of hay and from the railroad trestle into the flowing waters of the river below. We sat on tombstones in White's Cemetery at the end of the dirt road and tried cigarettes for the first time, choking and gagging and looking like our heads were on fire. We swam in New River and in any creek or pond that was at least waist deep. In winter we trekked to the beautiful sloping hills on Jackson's Farm that, when covered in snow, would rival any Thomas Kincaid painting. We would build a fire at the top of the hill and place potatoes and corn-on-the-cob our mother had wrapped in foil in the coals and let them cook while we rode the hood of a '53 Buick down the hill at breakneck speeds. When our gloved hands froze, we would pick up an ear of corn or a potato and roll it around in our hands until the feeling came back. After hours of sledding and dragging the Buick hood up the hill, the hot corn and potatoes made the best meals I've ever consumed.

Being the sons of a minister, we spent untold hours in church—Sunday school and morning worship, Sunday evening evangelistic services, Wednesday Family Training Hour, Friday night youth gatherings, and countless revivals, camp meetings, kids crusades, Vacation Bible Schools, and gospel singings. In those days "The Wonderful World of Disney" aired at seven o'clock on Sunday evenings. It was my heart's desire to relax in my pajamas after an already long day at church and watch a Disney movie; however, if we found ourselves at home on a Sunday evening, it was likely because we were too sick to recognize Mickey Mouse when he popped onto the screen.

Our lives were without much exposure to things that were profane or godless, only the usual hedonism that boys are attracted to—throwing a cuss word here and there to fit in with the crowd, trying those cigarettes in the cemetery, sneaking a peek at a girly magazine when hanging out with friends who weren't as sheltered as we were, shoplifting a Reese's Cup from the store down the road. But when the results of being caught participating in any of the heinous activities just mentioned is an old-fashioned lashing with your father's belt, one hesitates. Let me add, in my humble opinion, that I believe the lashings were acts of love as much as any hug or pat on the head. Today I bear no physical signs of the lashings but have carried with me all my life the education produced by them. To know my Father loved me enough to punish me when he saw signs of rebellion is invaluable. As a side note, *if* the lashings *were* a sign of love, it seems Dad loved Bruce much more than me.

Never in a million years could two brothers who grew

up like we did have imagined that the pathway of their lives would lead to the city of Atlanta and the worst neighborhood in the state of Georgia. We could never have conceived that the experiences of our childhood were preparing us for work that was more important than we could imagine, work that would often carry with it the import of life or death. When we dabbled with substances like tobacco and alcohol, we had no idea that we would one day invest so much into so many lives that had been taken prisoner by drugs and who were completely controlled by the addiction. There was no awareness when we peeked at horrible pornographic material that fifty years later we would be in the business of rescuing women and girls from the sordid world of prostitution, sex trafficking, and human slavery. When our parents spent all their time and resources tending to the poor and the "least of these," we didn't see it as training ground for what would come our way or as an example to follow. It was just what they did as people who had chosen ministry as a way of life.

When Bruce was seventeen, he sensed a calling to follow in our father's footsteps and enter the ministry. He didn't respond right away; rather, he spent a few more years sowing wild oats before finally giving in and becoming a youth pastor. At seventeen, I sensed a different calling and bailed out on God, faith, church, and everything holy. I was ready to watch as many Disney movies as possible. Eight years passed before I turned the corner and started to make my way back. I also became a youth pastor, and Bruce and I began our journey

29

of doing good works together, or at least simultaneously in different locations.

In 1997, Bruce was serving at a church in north Atlanta when he was given the six-month assignment to assess and suggest a plan for the future of a small struggling church in the city that was part of our denomination. It was projected that the church would be closed and the property sold as the congregation had dwindled to a miniscule number and there was no money to pay the bills. Ultimately, the building on 14th Street filled up with addicts, alcoholics, prostitutes, homeless people, and individuals returning to society from incarceration. Bruce realized that six months really meant the rest of his life. He describes it as being "conned by God." Thus, City of Refuge was born. The details of its origin can be found in Bruce's book, *Trust First.*[1]

In 1998, my family and I returned from our missions assignment in Jamaica and weren't quite sure what was next. I thought about returning to the school classroom as a teacher, something I did profoundly unsuccessfully for one year after college graduation, but I wasn't certified in Georgia and was not interested in going back to school as a student. I auditioned for pastoral positions at a couple of churches but wasn't feeling it. Finally, I called big brother. "Well," he said, "this thing in Atlanta is growing fast. Why don't you come help me with it for a few weeks until you figure out what you want to do."

---

1 Bruce Deel and Sara Grace, *Trust First: A True Story About the Power of Giving People Second Chances* (New York: Optimism Press, 2019).

30

I am now the Executive Director of City of Refuge South, but for twenty-four years, I helped Bruce, and for the first few years, spent considerable time contemplating what I wanted to do next. Sometime around 2008–2009, I began to realize that my calling was not to do something different in some other place, but to give my life to supporting my brother's vision and work. I started to better understand my role as a supporter, an armor-bearer, a right-hand-man. I settled into that role and have been absolutely fulfilled in life and work as a result.

I learned and embraced the fact that not everyone is given an Abraham-like or Moses-like vision and call to leadership; rather, the vast majority of us are called to follow and support those who are tapped to lead. Obedience to the call to follow, by the way, is just as important as obedience to the call to lead, because the most important thing is obedience.

A leader is not leading if no one is following, and a follower can't follow if there is no one to lead. Together as leader and follower we have responded to the homeless mother, the girl who has experienced sexual trauma since she was in grade school, the child who has grown up in the violent ghetto, the lost and wandering man recently released from incarceration, and many, many more.

We exist to bring Light, Hope, and Transformation.

Part 1

1
Roots

If you know where you are from, it will be harder
for people to stop you where you are going.
—Matshona Dhliwayo

....

THERE IS NO MORE suitable place to begin this story than from the singular soul and substance of Cecil and Dawn Deel. Without them, there is no story to tell.

This is not your usual acknowledgment of good parents who raised their children right and made sure they had ample opportunities. It is much deeper and wider than that. This is a complete attribution of credit to two people who lived their lives in a way that guaranteed their influence would carry on to the next generation. If there is an ounce of godliness in the Deel children, it is because of godly models and persistent prayers. If there is a drop of benevolence, it is because they were raised in an environment that had self-sacrifice for the sake of others at its foundation. If there exists a shred of capacity to forgive the offenses of others, it is because these parents demonstrated that there is no offense so great that forgiveness is not the appropriate response. If drawn to the poor, or angered by opportunity injustice, or sickened by discrimination, or disgusted by status-quo religion, or moved to action by the plight of defenseless women and children, Cecil and Dawn are to blame.

Our mother grew up along the banks of New River in the rolling hills of southwest Virginia and spent many hours during her teen years sitting by the river and praying that God would send her a husband. She prayed that he would be a man of deep spiritual devotion and that he would take her around the country and to foreign lands, where they would do the Lord's work together. In the spring of 1958, she learned that revival services would be conducted in the little country church her family attended, and that the evangelist was a young, single preacher from West Virginia. From the moment she heard the news, she knew the Lord had answered her prayers.

In early May, the revival commenced, and on the sixth of June, the day after her high school graduation, they were married. It was also her eighteenth birthday. They honeymooned for two nights at the Sands Motel in Dublin, Virginia, and had peanut butter crackers and a Pepsi for their wedding night meal. After borrowing money to put gas in Dad's '53 Ford, they hit the road and resumed the revival circuit, but this time as a team.

For the next fifty-nine years, Cecil and Dawn did life as life is supposed to be done. They lived simply, worked diligently, loved fiercely, parented responsibly, led with integrity, and followed obediently. Dad fulfilled Mom's dreams and was the answer to her prayers. With the deepest of devotion to God and humanity, they spread the Good News to the congregations they pastored and to the precious men, women, boys, and girls who populated the mission fields they traversed. They cared for "the least of these" as if "the least of these" were their own babies. They fed the hungry, clothed the naked, tended to widows and orphans, befriended the lonely, and viewed every egregious lawbreaker as someone who deserves another chance. They left their footprints in Virginia, West Virginia, Colorado, the Philippines, Korea, India, Haiti, Jamaica, Nicaragua, and the vast Native American lands of New Mexico and Arizona. Around the world people gather in houses of worship that our parents helped raise the funds to build, and people enjoy a quality of life they may never have known had they not crossed paths with Cecil and Dawn. Perhaps most important, their influence resulted in dozens of men and women deciding to enter the ministry and living it out the same way they did. The ripple effect is immeasurable. The depth and width and reach of their influence is greater than the river beside which Mom prayed.

When they found out their first child was on the way, Dad accepted a pastoral appointment at a tiny church in Duty, Virginia, just down the road from Richlands. In order to get Mom off the road and to be home like a good first-time father should be, he decided to settle down. In August 1960, Bruce was born. Benevolent blood continued to flow, and the world would never be the same.

When Bruce was just a few months old, my father's congregation expressed their overwhelming love and support for him and his young family with a Pastor Appreciation Offering of twenty-six cents. He was so moved by their gesture that he packed up the family and left. So much for settling down. He contacted the denominational powers-that-be and expressed his desire to be reassigned. There were no opportunities in the great state of Virginia, but they told him they had been informed by the powers-that-be in Colorado about a shortage of pastors at a few churches that had been planted during a missionary endeavor. It sounded adventurous, so off they went, with little Bruce in tow and a love lump in my mother's womb.

I arrived on the scene in September 1961, but my memory is fuzzy on the details. What I learned later is that I was the only one of four children who was born outside the state of Virginia, and I developed the assumption that, although I was not yet two years old when we returned to the Old Dominion, I occupied a special position in the family because of my geographical origin. Boy, did I have some things to learn.

Our father had moved his family of three from Virginia to Colorado to assume the pastorate of a small church in Fruita, not far from the hospital where I was born. My first home was a converted chicken coop in Loma, and it was there that I was initiated into life as the son of Cecil and Dawn Deel, and the younger brother of Bruce.

Mom once told us about the rail line that ran through Fruita, and how the trains would stop there for produce to be loaded, or for water or fuel. In those days, itinerants crisscrossed America in the box cars of those trains, and when the trains stopped, the ticketless travelers would jump out to find food, water, cigarettes, or other necessities and amenities. Many people saw them as a nuisance at best and a danger at worst, but my parents saw them as souls whom they could bless. They saw an opportunity to shed a little light in a dark spot by providing some refreshment to weary travelers. They began to pack lunches in brown paper sacks—peanut butter or a slice of bologna, potato sticks, and of course, a piece of fruit. Since bottled water had yet to be established as common fare in American culture, they carried a water bucket and dipper and washed the thirst from dusty throats. I think there's something in the Bible about that.

Thirty-five years later, after Bruce and I and the small army of folks who had decided to join us, started to address the needs of the homeless in Atlanta, one of our first efforts was to pack lunches in brown paper sacks and distribute them on the streets and under the bridges. As I sat at a table one day, assembling bologna and cheese sandwiches, my mother's story came to mind. *That's it*, I thought. *That's why we are compelled to make sure our neighbor is not hungry, or thirsty, or naked, or cold, or wandering aimlessly through life. IT'S IN OUR DNA!*

My thoughts ran through the years like a wild stallion, and the memories of the times our parents helped others swept over me, all the while wondering how we were going to get our next meal. I remembered the times Dad would preach until he was exhausted and drenched in sweat, and would be handed an envelope with his "offering" in it, only to give it back to the pastor on his way out of the door. His explanation was, "He needed it worse than I did." That had to have been a pretty serious need, we thought, as our stomachs growled.

I remembered when foreign missionaries came to visit or wrote letters requesting assistance, and how I never once heard my father say no. If he was asked, he would find a way to give something. Even in his waning years, when he had nothing extra to give, he would say yes to pastors and ministries in Africa, the Philippines, and the Native American reservations in the Southwest. After saying yes, he would call Bruce and tell him he had promised a financial gift to this ministry or that, but that he didn't have the money to send. He would instruct Bruce to send it for him because that was just as good. Of course, Bruce said yes. Every time.

The "Trust First" motto that Bruce lives by, and has built the City of Refuge (COR) model on, is not new to him, us, or the organization. It's part of the inheritance we received from Cecil and Dawn. The "We Say Yes" mantra, which is a pillar of COR philosophy and operations, is not something that was discovered in a think tank or brainstorming session; rather, it was woven into the fiber of the persons of Bruce and Jeff Deel from the time they were conceived. We didn't always pay attention to it, but it was always there.

I could tell a thousand stories to illustrate the willingness of our parents to sacrifice for the sake of others, but the night Mozelle Phillips called our house at a very late hour to say that her husband, Roger, was drunk and threatening to kill her again, should leave little doubt. Mozelle was terrified for herself as well as her two little girls, and she believed Roger was really going to follow through this time on his threat to end her life.

Dad drove the country road to their house and quietly collected Mozelle and the girls while Roger stomped around in the basement, cursing and screaming threats. Dad hustled them into his car and brought them to our house, which was the initiation of one of the most terrifying events of my childhood. After they arrived, the phone rang. It was Roger, drunk and belligerent, wanting to know if his family was with us. It was the one time I wished that Cecil Deel was capable of telling a lie, but he wasn't, and a few minutes later, the maniac showed up on our porch with a high-powered rifle. He fired a round into the air, which prompted Mom to drag us boys into the middle bedroom and cram us under the bed. For what seemed like hours, Roger Phillips stood on our front porch and shot his gun. He yelled and cussed and pulled the trigger over and over, but, thankfully, never shot into the house. Mom stayed on her knees by the bed for the duration of the episode, and as consistent as Roger was with his cussing and threatening, she was even more so with her prayerful intercession for the safety of her family, and his.

A Floyd County Sheriff's Deputy finally arrived and hauled Roger away in the back seat of his car. His parting words were that he would be back, and that my father would pay for stealing his wife and kids. He fulfilled fifty percent of his promise. At daybreak he was in our front yard, having already been released from jail. This time he had no gun but had brought his younger brother, Timmy, to use in an object lesson designed to teach Dad what he was going to do to him. He yelled for the preacher to come outside and watch and to be prepared for a subsequent "country ass whoopin'."

Dad walked onto the porch and observed as Roger picked Timmy up over his head and slammed him to the ground in the spirit of smackdown wrestling. As he started to lift the younger Phillips for another slam, Dad came off the porch and said, "Put the boy down and get outta here. You don't have a gun now, and I ain't no little kid. Now if you don't get outta here, you're gonna be the one that gets body slammed."

I was so hoping that Dad would counter with his own offering of ". . . a country ass whoopin'," but he wasn't capable of that either. Roger slinked to his truck and slid in on the passenger side. Timmy, more than happy to get out of there, jumped in behind the wheel and sped away in a cloud of dust. I wish I could say that was the last we saw of Roger Phillips, but it wasn't. He would pay an occasional visit to the church, usually after the service was over, and always drunk and nasty. He would spew all sorts of ugly accusations and challenge our father to fights on the gravel parking lot. On one of these occasions, Bruce and I went to the car and retrieved a couple of Coke bottles, the heavy glass kind, and snuck up behind Roger, ready to split his wig if things got real. However, Mom intercepted her little gladiators and told us to go wait in the car.

Roger Phillips was a menace to my dad, our family, and our church for the four years we were there, as well as a general nuisance to the rural community where we lived. He instigated many fights, terrorized his wife and kids, spun his car tires in the church parking lot, resulting in broken church windows from the flying gravel, and was in and out of jail. It seems the natural response would be to hold a grudge, or hope for calamity in his life, or at least to speak of him in tones of bitterness and disdain. But Cecil Deel never did any of that, nor did he ever speak disparagingly about anyone. When the subject of Roger Phillips came up, he spoke of him with compassion and empathy, always emphasizing his hope that Roger would one day "get right with God" and find freedom from the prison of his addiction.

It seems Dad understood that Roger's alcoholism and anger were only symptoms of much deeper problems, that his behavior was born out of his brokenness, and that he was really screaming for help because he was trapped. Perhaps he was angry at God, the church, and the ministry because of some disappointment he had experienced or hypocrisy he had witnessed. There was plenty of that kind of thing to go around, but I can't say for sure. What I do know is that our parents loved him in spite of his flaws, even when those flaws led to personal attacks on them.

Many years later, having pastored other churches and worked with thousands of people in missionary endeavors, Dad and Mom got word that Roger Phillips was on his death bed in Floyd, Virginia. Dad drove several hours to get to the hospital, praying along the way that Roger would still be alive when he arrived. He had a two-part mission in mind—to make sure the dying man knew that he held nothing against him, and to make sure he had gotten "right with God." Roger was still alive and coherent, and they had a great talk. Both parts of the mission were accomplished.

Looking back, our parents seemed to have always been attracted to the poor, the unattractive, the needy, the severely broken, and the poorly behaved, even if personal hostility was part of the experience. At the end of their lives, they had no bitterness to reconcile, no outstanding hostilities to account for, and no grudges to be carried with them out of this world. When sorting through word choices for their eulogies, *regret* was never given consideration. What a very satisfying way to live, and die.

It is from these roots that stories have grown like trees planted by streams of water, and they are still bringing forth fruit, in season. The stories are born out of obedience to a great sense of calling, inspiration from the greatest of all divine sources, and a lasting link to the legacy passed on by the best parents a person could ask for. Bruce and I grew up in an environment of protection, provision, and opportunity. We were shielded from harm and taught to work hard and be honest. We were blessed with a rock-solid family and had an abundance of positive role models, beginning with our parents. The vast majority of people we have worked with at City of Refuge for the past twenty-five years were born into something very different from what I just described. They have faced far greater obstacles than we ever imagined, and the result is that their stories contain a certain power that will stir hope in the most discouraged of hearts. They are the heroes; we're just the guides. Our upbringing prepared us for the task. We were never homeless or trafficked or addicted, but we were wired to be able to effectively work with those who are.

Our stories lead to their stories, and it is their stories that really matter. It is the City of Refuge stories that are most important here. I am compelled to describe how we grew up and how many of the things we experienced as kids and young men shaped us and prepared us for life and the work we do, but it is Anita and Jeremiah and Jennifer who deserve most of your attention. You will meet them shortly. I am driven to relate the importance of discovering your role in the world of leadership and followership, becoming comfortable with it, and experiencing the results of orderly teamwork, but the testimonies of people who have broken down barriers, gained momentum, and experienced transformation as a result of the process will teach the lessons better than me.

In the first psalm, the poet gives the perfect formula for having a life that is beautiful and productive:

Seek godly counsel and live by it.

Choose what is right and holy and pure.

Live a life of worship and service rather than profaneness and selfishness.

Consistently consume and meditate on the words of God, and do what he says.

These processes will establish healthy roots from which a beautiful tree of life will grow, a tree that will bless others with the shade it provides to worn and weary pilgrims. A tree that will point others to the perfect sources of provision and sustenance. A tree that will produce fruit that will bless the multitudes.

....

Cecil Burns Deel
March 20, 1937—May 14, 2017

Frances Dawn Landreth Deel
June 6, 1940—May 15, 2019

2

Formation

I met a boy whose eyes showed me that the past,
present, and future were all the same thing.
—Jennifer Elisabeth

....

It was there that we played basketball indoors for the first time, in a gymnasium that seemed ancient fifty years ago. We bounced a leather ball on a dusty parquet floor that was decorated with sole marks from sneakers and farm boots, attempting to avoid the dead spots that had formed during a thousand previous games. It was there that we heard Cecil Mabry sing *bbbbaby you just ain't seen nnnothin' yet* as he back-pedaled down the floor after making a lucky bank shot.

It was there that Miss Cherry told me to put my hands on the windowsill in her tiny office so she could exercise corporal punishment on my backside. In her sixth-grade social studies class, I had called a girl an ugly name, and Miss Cherry offered me a choice—ten whacks with her blue paddle with flowers painted on it, or a phone call to my parents. The decision was easy.

It was there that Bruce discovered a two-lane bowling alley in the school basement and was offered his first job. I don't know how the job description at the bowling alley read, but it could've been something like this: The pinsetter will duck behind a three-foot high wall and do his best to avoid serious injury or death from flying pins, followed by placing the pins back into the rack and resetting them. Repeat over and over until the game is finished. He made twenty-five cents per game.

Austinville Elementary School was at the center of much of our coming-of-age period of life. Bruce was in fifth grade and I was in fourth when our parents bought the first house they had ever owned, a small, stick-built structure in the miniscule community of Poplar Camp, just down the road from Austinville. During our first five years of school, we had moved four times, including a stint of living with relatives, each time transferring to a new school and starting over. Poplar Camp and Austinville Elementary School felt like home, and we settled into life as kids in a place of serenity. We stayed there five years, including transferring to Fort Chiswell High School at the end of our respective sixth grade years. This was the place where we learned important things about life and relationships, as the first significant friendships developed and enlightening experiences happened.

Much like certain diseases begin with one bad cell, our introduction to the profaneness of the world started on bus rides to and from school. The buses themselves were classrooms where we learned vocabulary we had never heard before. We also learned that vulgar expressions most often take the form of the spoken word but can sometimes be manifested in sign language as well, and we learned that acquaintance with the target of the expression is not a requirement.

It was there that we discovered a sandlot football field across the road from the school and learned that Austinville had its own team that competed against teams from three other communities in Wythe County—Max Meadows, Sheffey, and Ivanhoe. It was in the school gym and on that sandlot field that a love for sports and competition was initiated and great life lessons were learned. When we moved on to Fort Chiswell High, we continued to play ball at every opportunity, and a love for the outdoors and adventure became ingrained in us. In addition to the school and its amenities, the area where we lived was replete with natural beauty, historical significance, and local lore.

Dad paid $8500 for the little house on Brown Town Road in Poplar Camp, and we thought we had hit the big-time. The place was clean and wholesome, and we knew it was ours. I suppose knowing that we owned it gave us a sense that we would stay put for a while, and we did. At five years, it would end up being our longest tenured dwelling, but it took us about a day to discover that we had not yet reached heaven. Directly across the road was a green shingled house that was occupied by the Shepherd family, a ragged clan that could be pictured beside the word "dysfunction" in Webster's Dictionary. The Shepherds consisted of Ol' Man and Ol' Lady Shepherd (the only names I ever heard them called), as well as adult sons Gene and Joe, and Joe's children, Mike and Penny. Frankly, it was as if God had set us down, turned us around, and told us to look our future in the face. These were the kinds of people we would spend many years investing in and trying to help.

In the true spirit of family brokenness, Ol' Man Shepherd was still providing housing and food for two grown men in their forties who chose sitting in the yard drinking liquor and smoking cigarettes over working and supporting themselves. The real victims were Mike and Penny, who were already exhibiting the side effects of the irresponsibility of the adults who were charged with their care. Mike was in the same grade as Bruce and was perpetually in trouble at school, often being beaten by school personnel or sent home on suspension. He was the first person to offer us cigarettes, alcohol, and marijuana. On one occasion, he tried to get me to fill a plastic bag with hairspray and put it over my head to "huff" the aerosol. I was afraid to do it, but was more afraid of Mike, so I held my breath and acted like I'd had ice water poured down the back of my neck.

He bought the act.

Mike blew off two fingers playing with dynamite caps, wrecked his motorcycle multiple times, and was in more fights than anyone I knew, including taking a whooping from Bruce at school one day. It was several years after we left the area that I heard anything about Mike Shepherd, and it wasn't good. The husband of a woman he was messing around with caught them together and shot and killed them both. His sister, Penny, fared no better. She died a couple of years later from a gunshot wound inflicted by her own husband. Ol' Lady Shepherd died not long afterward, but who wouldn't?

Living in the shadows of temptation and evil influence made our parents more determined than ever to keep us on the straight and narrow. By far, the greatest institutional influencer in our lives as kids was the church. For the most part, we grew up in church, literally, spending a comparable amount of time there to what we did at home or school. The church was the hub of our life's wheel, and all other elements were spokes. Sundays consisted of Sunday school and morning worship, followed by an evening evangelistic service. Often, an afternoon gospel singing, prayer meeting, or homecoming took up the rest of the day. Sometimes we ate with church members. Sometimes we went home for lunch, but rarely. Sometimes we had a snack and a bottle of pop at the church building. Sometimes we starved. Weeknights were usually filled with prayer meetings, "Family Training Hour," church business meetings, and "Young People's Endeavor." Add to this recipe frequent revival meetings (that sometimes lasted two to three weeks), camp meetings, youth camps, and kids crusades, and there was enough church to lay a spiritual foundation that would last this lifetime and beyond.

The grandfather of the region where we grew up was the river. New River winds its way through southwest Virginia and touches the lives of everyone in the region. The river is like a wise old man that is full of history and quiet passion. It is not moved or shaken by new ideas or modern whims or economic development. As kids we spent untold hours by, or on, or in the river. Its waters have washed over us and been consumed by us. It was there that I learned to swim when Bruce tossed me from a little flat-bottomed boat and said, "It's time." To this day, I'm not sure if he meant time to swim, or time to leave this world, but I survived to tell the story. It was there that we took long naps when the fish weren't biting. It was there that creation became very important to us.

Not long after we moved away from Wythe County, construction of Interstate 77 began, and it crosses New River less than half a mile from where we lived. It's as if God saved us from its invasion, saved us from the giant steel and concrete monstrosity that replaced the modest Highway 52 bridge that seemed part of the natural landscape rather than an addition to it. I'm sure the interstate was a necessary part of progress, but it's never easy to watch as the fabric of one's youth is molested for any reason, at least if that fabric is serene and wholesome and pure.

One piece of history, and of our childhood, that has withstood flood, fire, and modern development is the Jackson Ferry Shot Tower. It is a seventy-five-foot-tall limestone structure that was constructed not long after the Revolutionary War ended. It stands within sight of the base of the I-77 overpass and a hundred feet from the river's edge. A builder named Thomas Jackson built the tower for the purpose of manufacturing ammunition for firearms. The war was over, but Jackson understood that pioneers and settlers would need guns and ammunition as part of their everyday lives. At the top of the tower, a firewood furnace was used to melt lead, which was then poured through a sieve and released in droplets that fell into large bowls of water at the bottom. The process of falling and landing in cold water caused the droplets to harden, forming solid lead "shot." It is a metaphor for our lives.

The ingredients and processes of one's childhood help to form the adult that is revealed later. In our case, the commitment of our parents to prepare us for the future was the tower in which we found safety and structure. The hardships and challenges we faced were like fire that made us fluid and pliable. The time would come when we would be launched out into the world toward the target of our purpose. These formative years would be crucial in making sure we were shaped properly and were hardened for the task. We would remain in the pouch for a season, but the time would come when we would be chosen to accomplish a life-long mission.

That old school building still stands in Austinville, though it has been closed for three decades. The sounds of children chatting at lunch tables, running the length and breadth of the old gym's parquet floor, and calling for the batter to swing on the baseball field, are only nostalgic memories. A few years back, we visited Virginia for a few days and drove to Austinville to see how it looked. I peered through the windows of the building and was struck by the sight of textbooks and papers still scattered in the classrooms. I tried unsuccessfully to locate Miss Cherry's blue paddle with flowers painted on it. I wanted to take it home and, in an act of poetic justice, burn it in my fire pit. To my surprise, when I tried the door to the school's basement, home of the notorious bowling alley, it opened. I stepped through the door and the memories came flooding back. I stood on a cracked and faded lane and entertained in my mind the sounds of balls landing on the hardwood and hurtling toward the pins like rolling thunder. I felt it and heard it and absorbed it again as if it were 1973.

As I started to leave the basement, fearing that a Wythe County sheriff's deputy would arrive at any moment, something against the back wall caught my eye. It was a solitary bowling pin, lying like a dead soldier in the area where the pinsetter worked. I went to it and picked it up, and to my surprise, it was still clean and very white, with only a couple of red stains that seemed to not be part of its design. *That's probably Bruce's blood*, I thought, so I took it home.

* * *

FORMATION

A life lived left of yesterday
The feelings vapor, the smells burning paper
The further I drift the less I know
Of bobbing on the ebb of days and dimensions of distance
Erasers of passions, thieves of sentiment, rogues of harmony
Epiphanous pilferers of breezes crossing shallow waters
Past wept out willows
Wafting through windows of musty gymnasiums
Swirling the dust from creaky parquet floors
And for a moment . . . leather

Asleep on a hay bed with snakeskin pillows
But rattled awake by time and space
Erasers of passions, thieves of sentiment
Usurping the sounds, sounds, sound of an anthem preaching
truth
"You ain't seen nothin' yet!"
But I don't want to see nothin' more than what I saw
Embezzled by time and space
Erasers of passions, thieves of sentiment
Like grains of sand falling, falling, fell
And left is the emptiness of time

—JEFF DEEL

3

Not Quite Right

If a man does not keep pace with his companions,
perhaps it is because he hears a different drummer.
Let him step to the music which he hears,
however measured or far away.
—HENRY DAVID THOREAU

....

GRANDMA LANDRETH was a beautifully simple and simply beautiful woman. She was meek and generous, kind and hardworking, faithful and devoted. When it came to our grandmother, you knew what to expect, and when you got what you expected, you were satisfied. Grandma was entirely satisfied with simplicity and lived in a way that minimized the world and its problems by focusing on her faith, her family, good food, and a home filled with life's basics. Her familiarity with the complicated, problem-plagued world came from watching *Days of Our Lives* and *As the World Turns* at 2:00 and 3:00 every weekday afternoon, but those were only depictions of someone else's misery, people she wished she could bring to her home so she could fix them. She would take them to tend the garden, or pick berries in the country, or to patch together a quilt with other beautiful and simple ladies at her church. After all, her love of God and his church, her devoted husband, Alvin, and her children and grandchildren, was more than enough to keep her cup overflowing. She was not one to make something of nothing or more of something than it actually was. Simplicity made for the best life; any unnecessary fluff only served to muddy the proverbial water.

Grandma Landreth was plain, in a way, but not in a way that would diminish her value to anyone who knew her. She didn't "put on airs," as they say, but she wasn't a useless lump of clay either. Because of her simplistic and straightforward approach to everything, Grandma saw no reason to view her grandchildren as anything other than what they were, or to call them anything other than what they were named. In her world, Bruce was Bruce, Todd was Todd, Vernon was Vernon, and so on. Among her gaggle of grandchildren, there were only two exceptions. Wilburn Doyle, Jr., son of my oldest aunt, Joyce, was nicknamed Buddy by his parents when he was an infant. Therefore, everyone called him Buddy because they had never known him as anything else.

The other exception was me. From the earliest of my memories, my grandmother never called me Jeff or Jeffrey, but Jeffy, which may not seem like a big deal, but it was really the *way* she said it that implied a purpose behind it. When she called my name, she looked at me like someone would look at a three-legged puppy or a one-eyed baby bunny. It was a look of pity and condolence. The tone of her voice was different when she spoke to, or about, me than it was when she spoke to the others. It dripped of commiseration and often sounded like she might burst into tears. The occasional use of the adjectives *little* and *purty* didn't help.

"That little Jeffy sure is a purty thing," she would declare to anyone who was listening, all the while rubbing my shocks of white hair like someone might do to an elderly relative on his deathbed.

I look back with great fondness on those days and the sound of her voice and her caresses, but when you are eight years old and surrounded by a passel of boys who purport toughness as the highest quality one can possess, being a purty little Jeffy can make for a challenging existence.

To make matters worse, my inclination that my grandmother viewed me as someone who was worthy of sympathetic affection was reinforced by other relatives. There was my Grandma Deel, who was a staunch woman with a stern look and direct manner. She was from deep in the hollows and hills of West Virginia, and she must've been taught as a child that language was only necessary when grunting or a slight nodding of the head or the pointing of a crooked finger could not possibly get the job done.

Aside from one statement I overheard during a visit to her home on the side of a mountain near Conklintown, I don't recall twenty words that Grandma Deel ever spoke. But that one statement stuck to me like a cocklebur on a shoelace. Bruce and I were playing in an upstairs room while the adults sat in high-back wooden chairs with wicker bottoms and listened to my grandfather, Henry Deel, talk. If Henry was in the room, he did all the talking, and everyone else did all the listening. Grandma did not like to sit on furniture, so she squatted in the corner of the room, her drab home-made smock hanging loosely around her, and watched us like a hawk on a wire preparing to swoop and make the kill.

As I tumbled near where she squatted and was getting back to my feet, in a gentle and worried tone, to no one in particular, she said, "Everything's not quite right with little Jeffrey, is it?" My mother heard the comment and rose system-atically from her chair, crossed the floor with resolve, scooped me up, and took me to the adjoining bedroom. She told me to stay there and sent Bruce to look after me.

Fast forward to my sixteenth birthday and my accom-panying informal initiation into manhood. Mom, a doppel-ganger to her mother, Grandma Landreth, presented me with a book: *Marching to the Beat of a Different Drummer.* With the same sympathetic expression Grandma Landreth exhibited, and that Grandma Deel wore when she drew the conclusion that everything was "not quite right," Mom gently rubbed my face and said, "You don't have to worry that you're not like everybody else, honey. God made you special, and he's going to take care of you."

She was right. And I think she was bitter toward Grandma Deel, because Mom wanted exclusive rights to declaring the specialness of her second son.

I went through school thinking I was smart, and I'm not sure why. It could be because I grabbed hold of every compliment or positive experience and used it as a definition for my entire educational journey. However, I found a few report cards in a storage container at my parents' house that provided proof that I was not part of the cream of the academic crop. I was a B/C student, with an A and a D dropped in here and there. As well, evidence would suggest that I was a student who gave plenty of reasons for my teachers to fill up the "Teacher Comments" section of the report card.

"Jeff needs to focus more."

"Jeff doesn't complete his assignments."

"Jeff makes sounds like the passing of wind during silent reading time." I'm not sure if I was dumb or just lazy. Probably a fine mixture of both.

The point of all this is not to be self-deprecating or to appear to be a weak and simple-minded imp; rather, it is to emphasize that although I was not looked upon as the shining star in my own clan, much less in the world at large, as life went on I became very comfortable in my own skin and came to understand that my contribution to the world could be just as valuable as the next guy's, if I could only find the wherewithal to accept my limitations. Among the throngs of children that have come into existence on planet Earth, a large percentage of them can be classified as "ordinary." They don't seem to have extravagant giftings or leadership skills. They don't win gold medals or MVP trophies. Their names never appear on the covers of books or magazines. But I believe that God looks at all of his creation and declares, "It is good." It is not about being the brightest star in the sky; it is about being the star you are and giving away the light that is within you. If that happens, your life will be a tremendous success. Mom was right—God has taken care of me.

For the first two decades of my life, I leaned heavily on my big brother for nearly everything. After all, the "not quite right" complex was deeply ingrained in my psyche, and I felt outmatched by the world. But upon college graduation in 1984, I found myself facing the inevitable challenge of having to forge my own way through life without Bruce standing in the wings ready to bail me out if I got in a tough spot, and I had not yet embraced my limitations. I had earned a degree in English and was ready to teach high school students about plot and theme and how to make their subjects and verbs agree. Bruce was working as a youth minister at a church in Florida, as well as coaching sports teams at the Christian school the church operated. He made me aware that the school had an opening for an English teacher, and when no one else would hire me, I applied for the position and found myself right back with him.

I don't know how many times Bruce apologized to school administrators for the recommendation, but it had to be a lot. After one year as Worst Teacher in America, an arrest that earned me forty hours of community service and a fourteen hundred dollar fine, and the discovery of alcoholic beverages in the house we were renting from the church, I was fired. The principal equated my maturity level to that of the students in my charge, but I'm sure the students would have been highly insulted by that comparison. Gone was my career pathway as an educator. Gone was my reputation among the people at the church and school. Gone was my chance to complete my community service hours right there at the church and school. Gone was my $135 per week take-home pay. I packed up and headed back to Tennessee. It was a tough time.

I tried working at the Boys and Girls Club, but my capacity to deal with unruly children was nonexistent. I decided to make a fortune as a caddy at an exclusive country club, but tripping on the first tee box and dumping the member's entire set of Taylor Made clubs onto the ground set the stage for a very short tenure. I hired on as a waterbed delivery and assembly guy and worked my way up to salesman, but I was blackballed when I wouldn't snort cocaine in the back room with the other employees, so I quit.

My efforts to make it on my own were monumentally unsuccessful.

Since Bruce was retained at the church and school in Florida, his association with me surprisingly overlooked, I had to figure out my next move. I contacted our grandparents in Pulaski, Virginia, and asked if I could stay with them for a while. They were happy to have me, and when I reached the little house on Thaxton Road, they had my bedroom set up and food in the fridge. Grandma was glad to have the chance to look after "little Jeffy" while he tried to find his way in life. I was twenty-five years old, and she still stood beside me as I sat at the kitchen table and rubbed my head.

I got a job stuffing crackers and candy bars into vending machines at Radford Army Ammunition Plant. After a few weeks, I was hired on as a line worker at the plant and began mixing explosives on the swing shift. That's right, the guy I've described to you so far—the Florida felon, the guy who drank Jack Daniels before heading off to teach high schoolers at the Christian school how to be good writers, the one who earned the consensus opinion as "not quite right," was now involved in a process that, with one small mistake, could make the entire town of Radford a memory. I was pouring a combination of chemicals into a giant mixer and turning them into propellant for fifty-caliber tank ammunition for the United States Army. It's only by the grace of God that Radford is still there.

In the meantime, the girl Bruce had pursued since he first laid eyes on her as a teenager at church camp finally gave in and married him, and they took another ministry position at a church in an Atlanta suburb. They met a young, single lady at the church, who was not looking for a husband, and brought her to Virginia to meet me, who was not looking for a wife. However, the minute I saw her, I decided that to look in her direction was a good idea.

After a seven-month and three days, long-distance, whirlwind dating relationship, we were married at her church in Georgia, but we decided to live in Pulaski so that I could

64

continue to risk my life and the lives of countless others for the benefit of a decent paycheck.

But Tracy couldn't manage Virginia. The winters were too cold and she was too far away from her mother. Five months of loneliness while I worked the swing, along with freezing days that kept her locked inside our small apartment, was all she could take. Not to mention the hardship of having me come home after eight hours at the arsenal, reeking of ether and acetone that no soap or body wash could remedy, trying to snuggle with my new bride. My bouquet may have been the proverbial straw that broke the camel's back, so we packed up and headed south.

I believe Providence had a lot to do with the move from Virginia to Georgia. I believe a woman was sent from down south to take me to my launch pad. She was the only person who could have convinced me to go. I was at least feigning contentment with my life and would have lived out my days working at the arsenal, or someplace like it, where there was the guarantee of a steady paycheck, insurance, and a retirement plan. I would have spent my off days climbing the mountains in my Jeep, fishing on Claytor Lake, hunting on Big Walker Mountain, and watching the dirt track races at Newbern. I would have replicated the lives of my grand-father and many uncles and cousins, men who have earned my deepest respect for their honesty and work ethic, and toward whom I direct no criticism. Had I stayed in Virginia, I would have lived a peaceful and wholesome life, but I would have missed my purpose, and I was too naïve and ignorant to recognize it on my own. Someone had to take me by the hand and challenge me to exit the comfort zone and step through a new doorway. As unwitting as it may have been, Tracy Deel was that person; she was my guide.

Although I consented to make the move to Georgia, I made it absolutely clear that I could not survive in a big city, so Atlanta was out of the question. I vowed that I would never live or work in that God-forsaken place, where there is more concrete than grass and where fifty percent of all drivers lose any sense of logic when it starts to sprinkle rain. Atlanta is busy and noisy, and I prefer tranquility and peace-and-quiet. In a true never-say-never scenario, I would end up working in Atlanta's inner city for a quarter of a century.

Tracy had spent the first fourteen years of her life in Augusta, Georgia, still had relatives there, and was familiar with the community. Not to mention, Bruce was there. A few months earlier, he had accepted a position at a church in Augusta and offered another affirmative voice as to why we should come. We made the move, and the wheels began to turn.

It began with my wife's insistence that we start attending church. I had not been a regular churchgoer since I left home and headed to college. I went often enough to qualify to play on the church athletic teams but not enough to make me a bona fide church fellow. She was adamant about wanting to have God and church at the center of our lives, and since my brother was on staff at a church down the street, I was without excuse.

If church did nothing else for me, it made me very uncomfortable with myself and how I was living. I was moving methodically through each day without goals, dreams, or purpose. I lacked motivation and found myself clawing and scraping for moments of satisfaction, and existing with an expectation that something great would one day fall in my lap, something I wouldn't have to work for. More and more, a great sense of unsettledness wrapped itself around me like a giant constrictor that increases pressure slowly until you can no longer breathe. I started to become desperate.

Denzel Washington once said, "If I'm going to fall, I'm going to fall forward." It must be nice to have a positive plan for when you fall. In my case, I fell to the lowest point in my life. I sank, really, into a deep and dark pit. Nothing was working as I expected it to. I was less than two years into marriage to a woman I loved but couldn't take care of. She had brought a two-year-old into the marriage with her, so the responsibilities of being a father had been there from the first day. Additionally, after moving to Augusta, we were blessed by the arrival of our second child, but another person to provide for increased the pressure even more. I had gone from being "not quite right" to not being right at all.

Something had to change. I had to return to my roots. I had to re-evaluate the loving proclamations of the matriarchs in my life that I was hearing a different drummer, that everything was "not quite right." Mothers and grandmothers have a powerful intuition when it comes to their children and grandchildren, and mine were on point as far as I was concerned. Each of them seemed to unwittingly confirm and support what the other two felt and believed. Oh, I was healthy and smart enough to get by, but it is to discover and live in one's purpose that makes for a complete and rewarding life, and I was never going to get there flying solo. The truth that was told to me when I was very young, by my leading female influencers, became guideposts as I dealt with the pressures that came with being a husband and father.

I am positive that my mother never once considered the prophetic move she made when she scooped me up off the floor at Grandma Deel's house and took me to another room and told my brother to look after me. Although she was coarse and a little scary, Grandma Deel was only offering her grandmotherly intuition, even if offering it while crouching in the corner. Her revelation seemed insulting, and it launched Mom into a mode of protection. However, I now see it as no different than Mom's "different drummer" assessment or Grandma Landreth's piteous labeling and head-rubbing.

Mom's decision to assign Bruce to be my leader and care-taker was a temporary solution, but looking back, it symbolizes what would be key to more than status quo living for both of her boys. At that moment, it was all about protection. As time went on, it would become a powerful leadership/ followership principle for living.

4

Fighting to
Learn to Fight

He who fights, can lose.
He who doesn't fight has already lost.
—BERTOLT BRECHT

....

MY MOTHER ALWAYS said I was a good kid, " . . . but that
smart mouth is gonna get you in trouble if you ain't careful,"
she added, occasionally. Being careful with my smart mouth
is something I did not learn to manage until I married a
woman with a mouth so smart it was as if her mouth graduated with honors from Harvard, while mine eked out an
Associate's Degree from West Bumble Community College.
The day after I said, "I do," my mouth gave up, at least in
any effort to compete with her. I humbly admit that I am
outmatched in this area of our relationship.

But before the days of husbandry, my smart mouth,
coupled with an innate ability to make people want to kill me,
led to many fights and verbal altercations. During my adolescent and teen years, I didn't mind starting fights; as a matter of
fact, I rather enjoyed it. I learned that, once punched a couple

of times, most of the boys we knew from school, church, or the communities we lived in would shrink to a pitiful state of surrender. There was plenty of talk to go around, but very little action when the proverbial rubber met the proverbial road. But there was another reason I didn't mind starting fights, or even losing them. I knew that my big brother was going to protect me from any real harm, and that he would be the one to retaliate, if retaliation was appropriate, and that I would ultimately have the last laugh, even if laughing through bloody lips. The pain and humiliation of a black eye or a busted nose here and there was worth it if the follow-up featured a TKO by my tag-team partner.

Of course, I am not a big fan of pain, so my best memories are the ones in which Bruce fought on my behalf before things got to the point of fisticuffs between me and whoever I was bothering at the moment. In these cases, it was obvious that I would suffer a pretty severe pounding if things proceeded, so Bruce would step in and take over. Once, he beat up a couple of boys at the same time for picking on me on the school bus. I'm pretty sure either of them could have single-handedly taken me, but he took them both. On another occasion, one of his best friends, Stephen, got weary of my smart mouth and invited me into the school bathroom to beat my you-know-what. He was a country boy who was taught that your word is your bond, and that if you say you're going to do something, you have to follow through and do it. He had said it, so he had to do it. Bruce showed up just before the pain began and convinced his buddy that it would be okay for him to take my place. They seemed to see the pseudo-altercation as an exercise in futility, so they only threw a few punches and quit, but at least Stephen walked away with his trustworthiness intact, though a little confused by the vicarious substitution.

Among the classic smart-mouth episodes is the time I was rescued by Bruce from our bus driver, who had me in a headlock that starved my brain of oxygen for three or four minutes. When I told my loving spouse this story, her response was, "Oh, so that's what happened." See what I mean about the smart mouth, magna cum laude?

I was a sophomore in high school and had boarded the bus for the afternoon ride home. Other kids were in line behind me, but I stopped in the aisle to chat with a friend near the front. The driver, a stout man in his twenties, told me to take a seat and clear the aisle, to which I responded, "I'll take a seat when I get good and ready. You just drive the bus and don't worry about what I'm doing."

The driver stood up and made his way through the other students, promptly throwing his arm around my neck, clamping down with all his strength, and calling me things I can't repeat. My ears burned from the pressure, as well as embarrassment, as I could faintly hear kids whooping and cheering. Then I heard Bruce's voice, "Let him go."

"What are you gonna do about it?" the driver sarcastically replied.

"I said let him go."

"Okay, but if I let *him* go, I'm gonna take 'hold of *you*."

"That's fine, but you *are* going to let him go, right now."
In one motion, the bus driver released my head and charged toward Bruce, attempting to grab him, but Bruce swung and caught him with a right to the jaw as he was advancing. The melee was on as they punched and wrestled for several minutes, eventually ending up on the floor between seats, each with a death grip on the other. It was hard to tell what was really going on, but the noise sounded like two bears at war in a burlap sack. Momentarily they figured out it was too difficult to try to fight while pinned beneath school bus seats.

I heard the bus driver say, "You good?"

"Yeah, I'm good," Bruce answered. They released their grips on each other and crawled from under the seats into the aisle. They both stood and dusted themselves off, Bruce taking his seat beside me and the driver proceeding to buckle up and head out on the route. The students lost their zeal as they realized the fight was over, and we had a calm ride home.

Those were the good old days. No weapons. No threats of retaliation. No gang violence. Just a little blood and a little dirt and an entertaining scrum between two kids and their bus driver. Neither parents nor school authorities had to know.

It's odd how the person who is most likely to kill you may also be the most likely to prevent others from killing you. I have often heard siblings say that they would fight each other like wild animals, but would band together in complete unity to prevent an outsider from harming the same loved ones they fought so terribly on a regular basis. It's not that Bruce was committed to making sure I never suffered; it just seemed that he wanted to make sure he was the originator of any suffering that came my way. It wasn't fair for someone who hadn't paid the daily price of having me for a brother to get the pleasure of inflicting pain on my person. Don't get me wrong—there were times, many times, when he put himself between me and trouble or pain, but there were also times when he saw the opportunity to implement a little torture, and at least once when he seemed to flip into the psychotic world of attempted murder.

It started over a pair of socks. Mom had brought a laundry basket of clean clothes to our room and left them for us to put away. I was diligently tending to my chore and had reached for a pair of my socks to put in the appropriate drawer, when Bruce grabbed the socks from my hand and said, "Those are mine."

"No, they're not," I said. "They're mine." I stepped toward him and snatched the socks back from him. This time he rose from the bed, grabbed me, and wrestled me to the floor. He forcibly took the socks, sat on the edge of the bed, and started to put my clean socks on his nasty feet. I knew I couldn't get the socks back this time, but I was furious and had to do something. I reached into the laundry basket and extracted a pair of underwear, white Fruit of the Looms, at least mostly white, knowing the entire time that I was making

73

a big mistake but fully committed to it anyway. I threw the underwear and watched with a combined sense of exhilaration and terror as they draped across his face. Although they were clean, in our tough-kid world, throwing tighty-whities on another boy's head was just plain unacceptable, and I had just thrown them on the toughest boy I knew.

When Bruce peeled the drawers from his face, to say there was rage in his eyes would serve to totally minimize the situation; it was some sort of murderous rage on steroids, like a grizzly bear you've just slapped with a stick of wood. I was instantly aware that the victory I had won in the laundry battle was not going to be worth the suffering that followed. He sprang from the edge of the bed and grabbed a pocket-knife from the top of the dresser, flipped the blade out, and started toward me. There was no time to think or consider options—all I could do was retreat until my back contacted the closet door. He raised the knife and thrust it toward my chest, and by pure reflex I threw up both hands to protect myself, my palms pointed outward, braced to absorb the cold steel. The tip of the blade landed in the center of my left palm, directly in front of my heart, barely breaking the skin and causing a little blood to gather, but not enough to fill a thimble. Bruce held the knife there and grabbed me by the chin with his other hand. "Don't ever do that again," he growled. "And if you tell Mom about the knife, well, I know where the knife is."

Love, devotion, and commitment are powerful elements

in a healthy family structure, but their presence does not guarantee the absence of conflict. If handled correctly, conflict can be equally powerful in establishing bonds that will last a lifetime, and beyond. It is through conflict that we learn how to deal with adversity, how to forgive, and how to heal. If conflict is handled properly, the parties involved are always stronger on the other side of forgiveness. The laundry incident caused our anger to burn hot, and we were not opposed to fighting it out, but the bond of brotherhood was always there as a barrier to any serious malice or harm. After it was over, I understood that, even in his anger, Bruce had no intention of plunging a knife into my heart. He stopped short of doing any real damage but went far enough to teach me to observe the boundaries of respect. I never again threw underwear on his head, and I expect I never will.

By the way, Mom never knew about the stabbing. You don't have to tell everything.

In so many ways, I think our relationship as kids was exactly what a relationship between brothers is supposed to be. I am acquainted with many people who have no relationship with their siblings, and even some who have not spoken to each other in years. It makes me very sad. If you are familiar with the Ten Commandments, you know that number five mandates us to honor our fathers and mothers. What better way to honor the people who gave us life than to love and cherish their other children? It is God's order to do so. Bitterness, resentment, jealousy, and anger are destructive emotions in any case, but when they exist inside the family structure, they are more shameful than in any other situation. Sadly, the reasons for strife between siblings are often petty, yet the ripple effect is monumental. The brokenness is passed on to the next generation as attitudes and conversations are strained through filters of resentment and bitterness.

Although I had no interest in fighting if big brother was not in the near vicinity, Bruce was satisfied to mix it up with others whether I was around or not. To be clear, he was not a person who picked fights or instigated trouble, but he was not going to back down if trouble showed up and called his name; that is, unless trouble toted a shotgun.

Our high school was embroiled in the standard football rivalry with the neighboring county, a territory replete with boys who tucked the legs of their Wranglers inside their farm boots and kept wads of Red Man chewing tobacco in their jaws. They drove noisy pickup trucks with rebel flags flying from the tailgates and "A Country Boy Will Survive" blaring from distorted speakers. Friday night football games between the two schools always included a few off-the-field skirmishes, some in the bleachers and some in the parking lot. On this particular Friday, a fierce altercation erupted after the game between a couple of rowdy rednecks from the visiting school and two tough-as-nails black kids from our clan. The fight was over in seconds, and the humbled visitors, with bruised and bloody bodies and smashed egos, were helped to their trucks by friends. The scoreboard read HOME 1, VISITORS 0.

But the corn-fed folks from Greene County were not about to take a beating from a couple of black kids from Charlottesville and act like nothing happened. At 3:30 Monday afternoon the bell rang and students from Albemarle High exited the building and headed to the buses and student parking lot, only to find twenty to thirty boys from Greene County waiting at the far side of the lot, their trucks running, flags flying, and "The South's Gonna Do It Again" pumping through someone's scratchy speakers. Boys from Albemarle began to set their book bags on the tops of cars and walk toward the trouble, gathering like a scene from *The Warriors*, until their numbers exceeded those of the visitors. One of those boys was Bruce.

On seeing the rapidly growing army of young men gathering across from them, one of the kids from Greene County ducked out of the line and went to a truck behind him. He emerged seconds later with a twelve-gauge pump-action shotgun into which he dropped several slugs. He walked briskly across the short divide between the two groups, and without hesitation, stuck the barrel of the gun under the chin of the first young man he came to.

"Do you want some?" he growled.

"No," the boy answered.

He moved to the next boy and repeated, "Do you want some?"

"No."

As he continued down the line, he received the same

answer each time he posed the question. The Albemarle army started to dissolve as boys left the line and defected to their cars. I suppose Bruce just had to feel the steel, as he waited until it was his turn to consider the question.

"Do you want some?"

"No."

The scoreboard read HOME 1, VISITORS 1. Game over.

For the most part, we spent our childhood in relative serenity, doing the things boys from mostly rural areas did in those days, and enjoying life with lots of good friends and a great family. But the reality of conflict has to be taken seriously in life or the humans involved will be blindsided when it comes calling. Bruce was not a troublemaker, but here and there trouble came looking for him, and he proved early on that he was not afraid of it. He pitched a kid across a table in the science lab, because the kid, a neighbor of ours from a highly dysfunctional family, would not shut up. The teacher, a frail and nervous little woman, went next door and retrieved Coach Goff, a burly tough-guy with forearms like Popeye and thick black hair growing from his knuckles. He brought his paddle with him and told Bruce to bend across the same table over which he had lofted Mike Sheppard. Like the leadoff hitter at that afternoon's baseball game, Coach Goff swung the paddle with both hands, lifting Bruce's feet off the ground with each whack. He winced, but never made a sound.

As we got older and ended up at the same college, I

continued to bother people and get myself into messes, and Bruce continued to bail me out, but looking back I realize that he was losing interest in petty skirmishes that his little brother created for him. He was always more mature than me, and the maturation accelerated as we became young men. Once, during a basketball game against former players from the university, I started to engage the smart mouth my mom had warned me about and ended up in a scuffle with the guy who was guarding me. Players from both teams began to chat and posture, until I came up with a solution that I thought was ingenious, but not everyone agreed.

"Okay, here's the deal," I said. "There's no need for all of us to brawl and have the cops show up" (I really didn't want to fight the guy because he would've killed me).

I continued, pointing at their six-foot-five-inch, 230-pound big man. "Bruce will take this guy out of town and find a field where they can fight. Bruce will whip his behind, toss him in the back of the truck, and bring him back."

I crossed my arms and waited for acknowledgment of my cleverness. I glanced at Bruce and knew immediately that he had a different idea. He wanted to take *me* out in the country and whip *my* behind. No one else liked my idea either, and the entire crew ended up in a nearby parking lot, and the cops showed up.

If memory serves me right, which is not always the case, I think that is the last time we mixed it up with outsiders in a way that could have led to serious trouble. I regularly thank

God that no one was ever seriously hurt or killed or imprisoned. On the other hand, I also give thanks for the lessons we learned that resulted from facing adversity and engaging in conflict. Some parents automatically act to resolve conflicts for their children, fearing that the child will lose, get physically hurt, or even worse, have their feelings bruised. In my opinion, and I am sure there will be opposing opinions, a child will be better equipped to deal with conflict as an adult if he gains a little experience along the way.

As a matter of fact, I am convinced that the battles Bruce and I had were training ground for what was coming in the future as we would spend our adult lives working with people in very messy situations. There is no advocacy for brawling or violence here, merely the suggestion that we can use the experiences from our youth, even the ones that resulted from our immaturity or stupidity, to make us better human beings in the future, and to thereby position us to more effectively serve our fellow man.

Our years at City of Refuge have presented us with droves of women and children who could not fight for themselves. Poverty, neglect, abandonment, abuse, addiction, or simply a lack of opportunity, had robbed them of strength, motivation, and resources. In many cases there was no hope unless someone showed up to go to battle on their behalf. Someone had to crawl in the ditch and attend to their wounds. Someone had to shine a light on their darkened pathway. Someone had to take them by the hand and help them find footing in their unstable world. Someone had to methodically restore hope in their hearts. Someone had to armor up and stand with them as they faced their dark enemies.

Someone had to fight.

5

Christmas 1969

Loss is part of life.
If you don't have loss, you don't grow.
—DOMINICK CRUZ

....

THAXTON ROAD is a narrow, hilly little thoroughfare that stretches less than two miles along the eastern edge of Pulaski, Virginia. Some of the fondest memories from my childhood are of visits to the home of my grandparents on Thaxton Road. It was a modest, two-story sandstone house on a small lot, with woods past a sloping backyard. The community was a quiet mixture of white families and black families in a time when people of different races mostly kept to themselves and mixed-race communities were rare.

Although close to downtown Pulaski, the area where my grandparents lived seemed rural and undeveloped, as if it was a settlement that was still being settled. It was replete with wildlife that was native to the area—deer, turkey, black bear, and small game—and beautiful hickory, oak, maple, dogwood, and fruit trees dotted the landscape. Laurel bushes lined every creek in the region, and wildflowers highlighted the roadsides and fields as if painted by God the day before.

My grandparents, Alvin and Josephine Landreth, were simple people who loved God, their family, and the United States of America. Grandpa worked at the local furniture factory for forty years, sanding the tops of dressers and chests-of-drawers until his hands were crooked with arthritis and his back bent like the blade on a sickle. Grandma kept house, made quilts, and cooked pinto beans and cornbread at the livestock market. They enjoyed picking wild berries to use for jellies and jams, and tending a garden that every spring and summer was flush with beautiful tomatoes, beans, peas, cucumbers, squash, peppers, potatoes, and much more.

Holidays were the best times to be on Thaxton Road. The sights, sounds, and smells of those times still ruminate in my mind like a good song that, once you've heard it, stays forever and demands that you hear it again once in a while. I am convinced that, in large part, I have not been trounced by the cares of life because I have a well of memories I can go to that always bring peace and satisfaction, and that quell anxiety and pressure. Memories of Thanksgiving at Grandma's house massage the tension out of my neck and the stress from my shoulders. It starts with the absolute magnificence of autumn in Virginia, with glorious fall colors covering the rolling hills and mountains. Frosty mornings give way to crisp days, and even when they are gray and the winds are blowing the leaves from the trees, the feeling is fresh and warm. Add the smells that emanated from the little stone house, smells of apple pie, homemade biscuits, cornbread, vegetables that had been canned the previous summer, and the best chocolate pies ever slapped on a human tongue, and you have life as perfect as it can be.

But my favorite holiday at Grandma's was Christmas. It was always cold, but the sights and sounds of the holiday, along with thirty warm bodies in the cozy confines at once, made the house as inviting as a campfire. The television was pushed aside in favor of a modest Christmas tree with mostly handmade decorations. Two chairs were placed to the side of the tree as seats of honor for Grandma and Grandpa Landreth, the most loved and respected people in the room. Everyone in the family revered our grandparents.

Christmas Day, 1969, started as the best of the eight Christmases I had experienced to date. Although I can remember only one gift from all the others combined—a bug-preserving chemistry set that I never learned how to use—I can tell you exactly what was under the tree on that memorable last Christmas of the decade of the sixties. Surprisingly, Bruce impressed Santa enough to receive a portable record player, complete with a tiny vinyl recording of the heroics of Johnny Appleseed. We had the story memorized before breakfast.

My individual gift was Fort Apache. It was a metal suitcase that was decorated on the outside with a western scene, including an 1800s-style Army fort with soldiers and Indians on horseback, engaged in a fierce battle. The suitcase opened to lay flat on the floor, revealing the inside of the fort, including plastic soldiers—some with guns and some with bayonets, Indians—some with tomahawks and some with bows and arrows, and horses—some in full gallop and some rearing up. It was the most exciting toy I'd ever seen, and I was immediately transported back to 1855, where I mounted my paint horse and galloped into battle, fully decorated in a feathered headdress and beaded chest protector. I preferred being an Indian; there was something romantic about it. Besides, Great-Grandma Lawson was one-fourth Cherokee.

When it was time to leave for my grandparents' house for Christmas dinner, I begged Mom to allow me to take the Fort Apache with me. "No," she said. "There will be too many people there and too much chaos. Your cousins will want to play with it and pieces will get lost." But I would not relent and continued to beg and promise that I would take care of it and not let anything happen. She finally gave in, and I couldn't wait to flaunt my new treasure in front of a dozen boy cousins.

As we began the twenty-mile journey to Pulaski where my grandparents lived, it started to snow. Many people dream of a white Christmas, and many more people sing with Bing Crosby about the dreaming. Winter in southwest Virginia almost always includes significant snowfall, and white Christmases were not foreign to us. Snow didn't stop people from coming and going; they just put snow chains on the rear tires of their cars and headed out into it. As kids, we would play in the snow until our hands, feet, and noses were frozen, then come in and stand by the fire, crying through the painful process of thawing out. Snow was part of our lives and to have it at Christmas time was the best, usually.

In those days, there were no Doppler radars or storm trackers, and it was hard to tell how much rain or snow was going to result from a weather system. You couldn't jump online to get updated; waiting for the evening news to come on and offer a sketchy forecast was the best you could hope for. Dad didn't put chains on our tires that morning because there were only a few flurries in the air and the trip was short. By the time we reached Grandma's house, there was a skiff on the ground, just enough to make things sloppy. It was a "wet snow," as they say, good for snow cream and rock-hard snowballs, but bad for tackling and wrestling. The first tumble in the half-frozen slush would result in clothes, shoes, and socks that were soaked through with no chance of them drying out for the rest of the day. Since our parents knew that tackling and wrestling were inevitable, we were made to go into the house to play.

The crowd was growing as each one of my mother's six siblings arrived with their spouses and children. As each new set came through the door, the commentary regarding the snowfall became more and more elaborate, and the elbow room grew slimmer. The snowfall had gotten heavier and was accumulating significantly on the ground outside. The hustle and bustle of activity inside the house continued as if it was a warm day in June or September.

I wasn't aware when the call came; I just remember that everything changed immediately and dramatically. The usual family Christmas atmosphere—gifts being carried in and placed under the tree, Uncle Ralph telling jokes at the dining room table, the ladies slicing ham and arranging chiffon and buttermilk pies on the buffet—was suddenly abated when my father rushed through the crowd with his long black coat hanging on one arm and disappeared through the front door into the snowy afternoon. In a moment, the noisy and festive atmosphere turned somber, the adults lowering their voices and shushing the children who were oblivious to the seriousness of the situation. I remember seeing my grandfather come down the short hallway from his bedroom, carrying their telephone in one hand, and the long cable attached to it in the other, and placing it on a small table next to the door that led to the basement. The phone was a heavy black device with a rotary dial, and I suppose it had been taken to the bedroom so my father could hear the caller away from the Christmas clamor.

Mom came into the living room and took Bruce and me by the hands and led us to the couch. We sat down in front of her, and she knelt and spoke softly. "Boys, your daddy had to leave because someone called and told him our house is on fire. I want you to sit here quietly and wait. And whisper a prayer if you want to."

I'm sure we had no idea what the implications of this news were, but I'm not sure the adults did either. There was not enough information to expect a certain thing or feel a certain way. We sat on the couch with our little brother, Keith, between us and wondered whether to be afraid or not, whether to be sad or just disappointed, or whether the outcome would call for neither sadness nor disappointment. Maybe the fire department would quickly put it out with little or no resulting damage or loss. Maybe the snow would extinguish the flames before they became too intense. Maybe the whole thing was a misunderstanding. Or maybe not.

As children, we didn't have the capacity to process the big challenges that life throws at earth's inhabitants. Our reactions to difficulty or loss were dictated by the adults in our lives; we followed their lead. We did what we were told, most of the time, by parents and teachers and other authorities. When we didn't, we usually ended up in trouble.

Heartbreak, poverty, disappointment, confusion, and uncertainty were constant ingredients in the recipe of our lives, and without leadership we would have been completely lost. Fortunately, we had leaders who would not let us down.

After a few minutes on the sofa, I crawled down and retrieved the Fort Apache from a corner by the TV. I folded it and snapped it shut, climbed back on the couch, and laid it across my lap, clutching it like an old woman gripping her bag while waiting on the bus. A couple of minutes passed, and I saw our cousins Todd and Brad come from the dining room where they had been taken by their mother, Aunt Gayle, when everyone started to realize something was wrong. Their usual rambunctiousness was gone, and they slowly walked over and climbed onto the couch and sat beside us and stared straight ahead without saying a word. No one asked when the meal would be ready. No one reached in an effort to play with the Fort Apache. No one laughed or goofed off. Five little boys just sat there, not knowing what to do, so we cried.

Brad, four years old at the time, began to rock, as was his usual habit. If he was sitting, he was rocking. He often wore a striped railroad conductor's hat, and the memories of him rocking with the hat perched on his little head are prominent in my mind. He started to rock slowly, and I heard sniffles coming from his direction. I didn't have to look to know he was crying. The sorrow, although for what we didn't really know, was contagious, and soon Todd and I were crying as well. Shortly, little Keith joined the mourning and cried like someone had eaten his Rice Krispies, his stuffed duck with the plastic beak held to the side of his face for comfort. I don't know if Bruce cried or not. I didn't look in his direction but kept my gaze forward and tried to muffle my sobs as best I could. If he wasn't crying, I surely did not want him to know that I was.

Momentarily, I noticed in my peripheral vision that Bruce reached over and ran his arm through the crook in Keith's arm, locking their arms together in a silent act of true brotherhood. It seemed right, so I reached to my right and left and locked arms with Keith and Todd. Todd looked down at my arm, and across at my brothers, and immediately reached over to lock arms with Brad. Brad continued to rock, pulling Todd's arm with him with each forward motion, but they remained part of the chain. For what seemed like hours, we sat on the couch and said nothing, but words were not required to bear one another's burdens. Our unwitting willingness to sit and cry with each other sent a strong message in every direction that none of us would ever have to walk alone. Through the years, the strength of the bond has been tested as our family has been rocked with brokenness, pain, and loss (especially the death of Todd and Brad's brother, Jonathan, at twenty-nine), but we have remained loyal to each other and have leaned heavily on each other when life gets nasty.

It was the next day before we knew the full extent of what happened to our home. Because of the snow, it had taken Dad more than two hours to travel the twenty miles from my grandparents' house to ours. He slid into ditches several times and had to be pushed out by other motorists, and was stranded behind an accident as well. By the time he arrived, there was nothing where the two-story farmhouse once stood except the back wall of the house, which collapsed as he walked into the yard as if it had been waiting for his arrival. Smoke trailed into the sky from bedsprings and other charred implements. Christmas lay in ruins.

Everything related to our family history was gone—photographs, keepsakes, school records, birth and marriage certificates, and a book manuscript my father had just completed and was planning to send to a publisher in the near future. The basketball, record player and Johnny Appleseed record, and the rest of the best Christmas we had ever had, along with the tree it came under, were all gone, lying in ash piles under the accumulating snow. By nightfall, the smoldering black spot on the ground was covered with eighteen inches of beautiful white powder.

Fort Apache was all that was left. The clothes on our backs, and Fort Apache. And love. And family.

The days, weeks, and months following the fire offered the greatest learning experiences of my childhood—not learning in the sense of academic education, but learning about the substance of the human heart and the capabilities for kindness and meanness, generosity and selfishness, compassion and cynicism, that lie there.

There was an outpouring of care and support from neighbors, family members, and friends that was both heartwarming and practically beneficial. We received gifts of clothing, hygiene products, and money. But some people saw us as a better option than the dumpster for garbage from their garages and basements. Specifically, I remember being excited to receive a few pairs of pants that were exactly my size, only to discover stains that could not be extracted. In the same box were sneakers with loose soles that flapped with every step, and a few pairs of used underwear, which, in my humble opinion, is an absolute no-no.

I also remember receiving some cool new toys in the donations, but I can't remember exactly what they were. The ones I do remember are the model cars that were missing a few parts, the stuffed animals that were dingy and smelled like saliva, and the giant Styrofoam T-Rex that Bruce and I were very excited about until we realized it only had one leg and would not stand up. It is quite anti-climactic to finish constructing a six-foot dinosaur, only to realize all it can do is lie on the ground like a sleeping dog or lean against the house.

Some things transcend time and space, and the act of unloading garbage on the needy in the name of benevolence is one of them. A few years ago, at City of Refuge, we stopped accepting the donation of used clothes because of the enormous task of separating the usable from the unusable. It is unfortunate for the people who wish to donate good items that our folks could actually use, but we couldn't manage it. Back in the days when we would accept almost anything, we have opened boxes to find stained and dirty clothing, dishes that had not been washed, toys that I'm sure had been in a classroom for three-year-olds for a few years, and even a stripper's outfit (I will spare you the details).

I am profoundly grateful to the people who generously blessed our family during a very trying season. As well, I am always grateful when people display generosity in practical ways and with a spirit of excellence at the heart of it. As a side note, the best blessings do not always come from sources you might expect. During our time of crisis, total strangers helped to make sure our needs were met, and neighbors we barely knew stepped up with surprising generosity. On the other hand, there were relatives and close friends who simply said, "We'll be praying for you," or who just ignored us altogether.

The most egregious behavior came from—are you ready?—members of the church my father was pastoring at the time. The church decided to build a new parsonage for us, and upon completion, the Ladies Ministries department put on a housewarming shower. After presenting Mom with dozens of gifts—dishes, pots and pans, towels, decorations, and practically everything else you would need to set up housekeeping—the president of the group rose and made the announcement that every gift that had been given was the property of the church. She made it clear that, although my mother had lost everything she owned, the efforts of her fellow church members would be directed only toward their own self-interests. The excitement and anticipation of moving into a brand-new brick house, filled with sparkling new amenities, fizzled like dying fireworks.

Not long after that, we left them with their new flatware and coffee mugs and moved on.

I was only eight years old when the fire took our home and everything we owned, but I learned lessons from the experience that have remained with me through the years. I learned that focusing on the things that are most important in life—love and family and bearing one another's burdens—will sustain you during periods of profound tragedy and disappointment. I learned that stuff can be replaced, but that selfishness can rob you of relationships and productivity. I learned that there is both kindness and cruelty in the world, and that neither of them should take us by surprise. There is no question as to whether they exist; the question is: *How will we respond when they show up?* I learned that benevolence must have at its core a spirit of excellence or it's not benevolence at all; rather, it is only an obligatory gesture.

These lessons would prove to be profoundly important as our life's work unfolded before us and we began to encounter people who had lost everything, including love and family and friends. People who had been robbed of dignity and self-worth showed up on our doorstep on a regular basis, people who had been the victims of life's fires and whose existence now amounted to a smoldering spot on the ground. In some cases, they needed a comfortable place to rest for a while and good food to put in their stomachs, and they were soon back on their feet. In other cases, they needed long-term care, counseling, and vocational training. In all cases, they needed prayer, love, and family.

6

On a Hillside
in Roanoke

Love and compassion are necessities, not luxuries.
Without them, humanity cannot survive.
—Dalai Lama

....

THE MIGRATION STARTED in early June, the kids newly released
from the torture chambers of public, private, and Christian
schools, their spirits soaring and their bodies energized for all
that Youth Camp would have to offer. They had been cooped
up in musty classrooms and on dank cheese wagons and in
mildew-infested locker rooms, and they had dreamed since
Christmas break of the moment when that bell, the one that
had jolted them out of daydreams and half-slumbers every
fifty minutes of each school day for the past nine months,
would ring one last time, dismissing them not only for that
day, but for the next ten weeks.

They came by bus and car and the notorious church
van. Like hungry ants converging from all directions with the
promise of piles of sugar waiting at the journey's end, the kids
and their adult chaperones made their way to the campground.

The vehicles rolled down country roads and state highways like so many streams navigating from all directions to the same river, pushing their way to Interstate 81 and eventually to Exit 146 at Plantation Road. And there it was—Almighty God's home-away-from-home in the state of Virginia—the Church of God campground.

For many of us, a certain feeling accompanied that first glimpse of the campground as it came into view from I-81, a feeling that remained until the scenery faded from view as we departed at the end of the week, but sometimes it lingered for days afterward. Even now, nearly half a century later, a tinge of that feeling, although diluted by time and distance, will waft over my senses as I have some recollection of those days. It is a feeling that has wonder at its core and is layered with memories that bring laughter and tears, an undying love for people who probably don't remember my name, an abiding influence that shows up in so many aspects of life, and a deep, unexplainable sense of spirituality.

It is hard to articulate how a few weeks at summer camp could have an impact that would affect a person's worldview and life's work, but that is what happened to us. In retrospect, I suppose we learned so many things that, at the time, we didn't know we were learning—important things that were shaping the way we made decisions, the way we cultivated and maintained relationships and organized priorities. Going to camp offered our first glimpse of life outside the govern-ment of our parents' home and the local church our father pastored. We were blessed with wonderful parents who loved us and took great care of us, but we were sheltered, to say the least.

Folks who have never attended a Christian camp may think everything from the kitchen sink to the pillow talk after lights-out was squeaky clean, but those folks would be wrong. Not every camper adhered to the strict standard of Christianity we were accustomed to. Some of the other campers were the children of preachers, but most were coming from "normal" families that were living and working in the real world. They may have been regular church attenders or they may have been recruited with the idea that church camp would be the vehicle that would lead to the salvation of their souls. Or, they may have been outright reprobates who came to camp to escape their crappy home lives for a few days or were sent by parents looking for an opportunity to unload them for a week. It was a giant mixing bowl of people who brought their own flavors and colors to the camp experience. It was the kingdom of God and the kingdom of darkness all at the same time.

Youth Camp was a summer festival of fun and memory-making and spiritual renewal. It was flavored by all of us who were part of it, from the State Youth Director, who branded our hearts with his compassion and wisdom, to the counselors who were subjected to spoiled brats and sleepless nights, to every kid that had camp as part of his summer break, even Kenny from Richmond who wore an AC/DC shirt the entire week and who is the only kid I remember who held out on all the invitations for salvation. I hope he's okay today. He was fond of walking around his dorm room and the bath house in his AC/DC shirt, but with nothing on from the waist down. I really hope he's okay.

Youth Camp was a culture that consisted of bright, funny, good-looking guys like Steve and beautiful, creative, magnetic girls like Lynn. It was a haven for great amateur athletes like Keith and Darrell and a gathering ground for wholesome, down-to-earth girls like Teresa and Alice. But it was also a place where kids who had home lives that were characterized by poverty, addiction, and brokenness came to escape their dark corners and find a little light and love. It was a place where outcasts were treated with value and the less-thans discovered they were enough. It was a family with a cast of members that included the full range of humanity. It was all of us.

Our time at camp revealed to us, both while we were there and as time went on, that there was a world outside the bubble and that we had a tremendous responsibility to love and care for the people who occupied that world. We had to escape the bubble. The paradox of going to a church camp to learn that people outside the church need us just as much, or maybe more, than people inside was a game-changer. At camp, we saw the results of abuse, neglect, and abandonment. We met kids who were dealing with the fallout of addiction in their families and kids who were living in the throes of extreme poverty. We had no idea how to help, but we were being prepared for the future. We learned that it was good to gather around our hurting friends at the designated times, and to weep with and pray for them, but that those exercises were often not enough. Some of them would need a friend who cared enough to join them on their difficult journey.

Just because it was a Christian atmosphere and was operated by a religious denomination does not mean that everyone there was living in a deep relationship with God and embracing his purpose for their lives. The hillside in Roanoke was home to church services, Bible studies, and worship music, but it was also a rest stop for weary young travelers who needed respite from family fights or the barrage of pressures that pelted them every day. In other words, the kids with whom we attended Youth Camp were from the world and not just the church, and they went on to become adults who reflect the general population and represent humanity at large. Bruce and I were blessed to be thrown into the camp melting pot for a few weeks each summer, and I can now see the difference it made in our worldview. God created his children to live in community and to love and care for the people around us, especially those who are hurting.

Youth Camp offered us refreshing reminders that God loves people who are imperfect, people whose lives are characterized by victories but also by failures. People who do everything right today but screw it up tomorrow. Those weeks relieved us from the fear of being cast out of God's family if we had a bad thought, said a bad word, or caved in when temptation showed up. There were times when we became so frustrated with our inability to live up to the standard of "holiness" that was presented to us, and demanded of us, that we finally gave up trying and settled into deep pits of rebellion.

As good as their intentions may have been, some of the preachers who stood in our church's pulpit brought not only the Word of God but truckloads of condemnation with it. On one occasion, a traveling evangelist named Perry visited our church and preached a few times. Reverend Perry was a nice man but had an unfair advantage when it came to pounding on his listeners with the hammer of God's wrath and judgment. He was cockeyed, which made it virtually impossible to know to whom his words were specifically directed, if anyone. One eye pointed east and the other pointed west, and the effect was unnerving. At the end of one sermon, he told the story of a young man who attended a recent service and was warned by Reverend Perry that he was facing his last opportunity for salvation. The boy ignored the warning and left the building. While walking home, he was struck by a dump truck and killed, or as the reverend put it, ". . . went out into eternity lost and undone without God."

Bruce and I sat on the back pew and listened to the story, absorbing the warning as our own and shrinking under the piercing eye of the preacher. When he gave the invitation for salvation, we rose and sprinted to the front, falling on our knees and crying out for forgiveness. We begged God to not send us out "lost and undone" because of the poker cards we had hidden in our bedroom, or the sips we had taken from Claude Graves' bottle of apple wine at the previous week's football game, or the magazine we had looked at when we were at Kevin McPeak's house one day after school. We arranged with the Almighty that we would forsake all such activity and burn the paraphernalia if he would agree to keep the dump trucks away.

Later that night, as we visited over Pepsi and sandwiches, Reverend Perry expressed how proud it made him that we responded to the call and made things right with the Lord. "I didn't expect it from the pastor's young'uns," he said.

"We didn't feel like we had a choice," Bruce responded. "You were looking right at us while you told that awful story."

"Boys, I didn't even notice y'all were back there until you came running down the aisle. The message was for a young lady on the other side of the room. I was talking to her."

We lay in bed that night and discussed how we had been the victims of cockeyed salvation. We concluded that there was no way it would stick if we were not the intended target. We tried to reconcile the possibility that the young man whose life came to a terrible end on the bumper of a dump truck left the service oblivious to the fact that Reverend Perry was talking to him. Perhaps he would have responded to the call had he known he was the target. Perhaps there were multitudes of people out there in the world who had been victimized by the preacher's unfair outlook.

Bruce offered the final word on our confusion. "Well, little brother," he whispered. "We're going to hell anyway; we may as well enjoy the journey."

Although there were many similar experiences, Youth Camp opened the floodgates of grace and freedom as we spent time in the company of people who cussed when a wasp stung them, or peeked through the cracks in the fence during girls' swim time, or broke into the concession stand in the middle of the night for a drink and snack. Yet, when confronted with the love and forgiveness of God during the evening service, they would melt into the arms of the brothers and sisters around them and weep out their repentance. We came to understand that God loves people whose lives are broken, whose minds are confused, and whose actions are the result as much as he loves the person with pristine behavior. The grace we discovered has helped us to navigate our way through the entangling webs that religion can sometimes cast over the beautiful experience of placing one's faith in God.

Among the throngs of beautiful individuals we had the privilege of attending camp with, perhaps the most memorable and influential was a boy from Alexandria named Matt Willetts. To those of us who had lived sheltered lives, Matt was an explosion of creative energy that my grandmother would have called "sacrilegious." He was familiar with movies that contained curse words and love scenes and profane comedy, material the holiness crowd we were familiar with would have declared had its birthplace in hell. When he talked about

Saturday Night Live, I nodded agreeably and feigned laughter because I had no idea what it was. The show was brand new in those days, and we were not allowed to stay up that late or to watch shows that included off-color material. Having seen the show once or twice since then, I have no doubt that Matt could have been a regular, had that been his goal.

The night Matt showed up at Fun Time after a Youth Camp service, dressed like an Egyptian pharaoh and gyrating to the music of King Tut, I laughed so hard I thought my sides would split open. I learned that some guy named Steve Martin was Matt's comedy hero, and once I became familiar with Martin's work, it struck me that Matt was every bit as good at comedy as Martin, and as good as all the pros.

Early on, Bruce and Matt became good friends, although they were vastly different in nearly every way. Bruce was a leader then and still is now. Matt was a leader as well, but he was flamboyant, arrogant, noisy, and obnoxious. Bruce was willing to take the dive and to influence others to dive with him, but he did so in a more mature and methodical way. They were a match made in heaven. The rest of us were like Thaddeus and James the Less from the list of Jesus's followers, no-namers just looking for someone to follow. Matt and Bruce were Simon Peter and John the Beloved.

Matt Willetts, like us, was the son of a preacher. His parents pastored small Pentecostal churches like ours did, but if we were pinto beans and cornbread, they were Cracker Jacks and cotton candy. He was the only boy among five siblings, and the entire family was artsy, musically talented, and funny. They brought life and energy we had not seen before to the Youth Camp experience. They performed skits, told jokes, and led us in raucous singing, all while maintaining respect for God and camp rules. As stupid as it sounds, and was, singing "I like to eat, eat, eat eeples and baneenees" at the top of our lungs was a welcomed diversion from the mundaneness of the church life we were used to. In other words, they were not afraid to have fun and perpetuated a message that God doesn't mind it either. When it came time to pray, they were among the first ones to wrap their arms around you and share your burdens. When it came time to worship, they were up front, giving of their talent and leading the rest of us. But when the Fun Time hour arrived, watch out.

We forged a friendship with Matt Willetts that continued long after the glory days of Youth Camp ended. After high school graduation, Bruce and Matt both chose Lee College in Tennessee for their post-secondary pursuits. The school, now Lee University, is a thriving liberal arts institution, but in those days, it was a small college that focused mainly on ministerial training. Matt lit up the Lee campus like he lit up the campground. I arrived a year later and began the next phase of my educational journey, which mostly amounted to following the two of them around and acting cool.

The "Matt stories," as we call them, still make me weak when I hear them, or tell them, and they have been a source of life-fuel for decades. He is included in this book because of his undying influence on us, and I aim to keep him alive because his life was much too valuable to remain encased in a three-paragraph obituary. He gave too much to the world for the world to forget him.

As we lay on our bunks at Youth Camp in the late seventies, or in our dorm rooms or apartments at Lee in the early eighties, none of us had any idea that the days ahead would hold such pain, and that we would walk the painful journey together. In our collective imaginations, we could never have dreamed that the beautiful creature who made us laugh more than anyone on earth would leave so soon and create chasms in us that could never be filled. We were young and we were having a blast. I, for one, was narrow-minded enough to believe things would always be that way.

But life happens, and it brings disappointment, loss, and pain. The question is whether or not we will allow the ugly fallout from these experiences to bury the love, laughter, and life that we, also, have been blessed to experience. We can spend our lives in dungeons of depression because hurt has shown up as a joy robber and a peace thief, but we have the choice to do what I'm doing now—keep the laughter alive, throw more wood on the memory fires, allow the good experiences with family and friends to fill us up when the tank nears empty.

When Matt was fighting for his life, it was Bruce who dropped whatever responsibilities were on his plate, took the time, drove the miles, and did the work to make sure Matt

107

had a friend at his side. It was Bruce who made sure Matt had someone to laugh at his jokes, someone to encourage his sisters, someone to shoo away the cuckoo birds. To the very end, Bruce was there, and was there to extend great honor to his friend and brother at the memorial service.

But it all goes back to a hillside in Roanoke, where friendships were started and lessons were learned that helped to set the course for our lives. Matt Willetts was one of those friends, and although he died at age thirty-three, he is still hanging out in our hearts and minds nearly thirty years later. His life was like a stained-glass window that was created by a master artist. Once broken, it could never be duplicated, but I'm thankful that he left some of the beautiful color with us.

Matt may have been the most memorable and influential person from Youth Camp days, but he was only one of many who left their indelible mark on us. Ironically, we spent over nine months of the year in school, and only three or four weeks at camp, but the memories from camp, including the people who are part of those memories, monumentally outweigh those from school. When we left that campground for the last time as young men, the experiences from the campground did not leave us. They remain today as part of the substance of who we are.

7

Follow the Leader

Can two walk together, unless they are agreed?
—Amos 3:3

··

OF ALL THE STORIES that constitute our lives, a few have been
kept alive, perhaps for posterity, or perhaps there is a timeless
lesson buried in the story that never loses its relevance, or
perhaps both. To be sure, every story our parents and other
relatives passed down to us or kept alive through the years
still bears meaning today; thus, we pass them on. In the case
of Bruce and me, every story is a leadership and followership
story. It is the design of our lives and we have lived inside the
design without complaint. It goes back to the early sixties
when we were living in Suffolk, Virginia, at ages three and
two. After returning from Colorado, Dad accepted a pastoral
appointment at a small church in Suffolk. It was a two-story
building with our living quarters upstairs and the church
sanctuary downstairs. It was situated in a crowded neighborhood, and we had no yard to play in and were confined to
the building most of the time. At some point, Bruce, at three
years of age and already brimming with a spirit of adventure,
began to plan our escape.

In those days, we had no television to which our eyes and attention were glued for untold hours, no video games, and no computers or tablets. We, and most all the kids we knew, were provided with a handful of playthings and left to use our imaginations to learn, build, carry on relationships, create and resolve conflicts, and engage in competition. But sometimes an inner desire to push beyond the boundaries of normal play would rise up, or boredom would take over, or an intense drive to explore would supersede the drive to build another cabin from Lincoln Logs or to create a new look on the Mr. Potato Head. I suppose that's what happened on this particular day.

As our mother moved about the house, busy with the usual household chores, Bruce waited for a moment when we were unsupervised, and like tiny convicts with one eye on the guard and the other on the gate, we snuck out of the house. According to our mother, we left the door standing open and could be heard squealing as we discovered an outdoors saturated in an afternoon downpour, so we were not hard to find. The usual panic that strikes a parent when a small child disappears for even a moment was short-lived in this case as Mom quickly located us running circles around the house in the pouring rain, stopping at buckets that had been strategically placed to catch water, and splashing ourselves and each other like we were at the beach. Bruce got spanked and I didn't. The experience foreshadowed the entirety of our childhood from that moment forward.

As a young man I followed Bruce into the realm of the heathen. I suppose we had to get it out of our systems, so we dove into a lifestyle of partying as if we knew what we were doing. We smoked Kent Golden Light cigarettes and drank our fair share of beer. When we had a little extra money, we drank Heineken, and when we were impoverished, which was most of the time, we drank Milwaukee's Best. After all, the price for a case of Best was about the same as for a six-pack of Heineken. After a season of sowing wild oats, Bruce, having decided it was time to take life more seriously, rose without notice one day on the rooftop of our garage, dropped his Kent Golden Light into his beer can, and crushed it on the railing. "Well," he announced, "I reckon I'm done with that." He never drank or smoked again.

I followed Bruce from the pagan world of smoking and drinking to a more serious and sacred lifestyle, but it took some time. He took off for Louisiana under the presupposition of working in a church but was mainly used as a delivery boy for the pastor's cash-only furniture business. I sat with the smokes and beers for a while longer, not making the journey back to responsible living until I was twenty-six and married.

At thirty-seven years of age, I followed Bruce to Atlanta's worst neighborhood, not knowing why or what the future would hold. What I did know was that I could depend on him and he could depend on me. To this point, the pattern of following my brother was not intentional. I was not aware of the fact that I had been launched into my purpose and that the rest of my life would be characterized by followership. I was sure that I was in training to lead my own ministry, pastor my own church, do my own thing. I did not feel like leadership material, but I was confident that I could be trained up and developed and would be set forth at the appropriate time. What I learned, after seven or eight years of expectation that everything I was doing was preparing me to break free and lead, was that I was actually in training to be a swing dog.

On a dogsled team, the swing dog occupies the spot right behind the leader. The role of the lead dog is to steer the team and set the pace. The swing dog is taught to pick up signals and messages from the leader and to influence the rest of the team to do what the leader wants. If it is to continue on a straight pathway, the swing dog will keep the others in line. If the leader signals a turn to the left or right, the swing dog will ease out and let the team know they will be "swinging" that way. If danger lies ahead and the team needs to slow down or stop, the responsibility falls on the swing dog to ease the team back in order to avoid a chaotic pileup.

It is an ideal picture of leadership/followership teamwork. For twenty-five years, Bruce has cast vision, steered the team that surrounds him, and set the pace. He has plowed ahead on a run that he knows will take the rest of his life. When I joined him one year into the journey, neither of us knew that I was assuming the role of swing dog and that I would serve to pick up his messages and signals, passing them on to the team, and I would make sure we stayed true to the mission. Bruce calls me the "culture caretaker" for the organization, the person who sounds the warning when we start to make a wrong turn, the person who understands the intentions and motivations of the lead dog better than anyone else. I am the guy who notices and calls into account people or things or ideas that are contrary to the spirit of who we are and what we are called to do. Sixty years of following the leader have positioned me to know what the lead dog will do before he does it, to know what he wants before he expresses it.

This leadership/followership teamwork has not only kept us on the right pathway and moving in the right direction, but from time to time has been vital to our basic survival. It hasn't always been smooth sailing.

We have dealt with naysayers, financial challenges, distractions, disappointments, and issues in our own nuclear families. We have at times suffered from blurred vision and a misalignment of priorities, but Bruce has never stopped leading, and I have never stopped following.

In the summer of 2019, City of Refuge was basking in a limelight of notoriety and success in Atlanta and was starting to get the attention of leaders in other cities as well. Financial support was strong and stories about our work were appearing regularly in news releases generated by the leading media outlets in the city. Bruce had been asked to write a book and it was being endorsed and promoted by nationally known figures. He was receiving invitations to speak at corporate, church, and civic events, and he was being offered significant money to go on a speaking tour. Times were good.

Six weeks later, Bruce and I met for hours in his office to discuss the future of the organization, even digging into the possibility that City of Refuge might be forced to dissolve, and ruminating about what we would do next if that happened. Just days after the official book launch in July, an event that was attended by Atlanta city officials, corporate leaders, and major influencers from New York, we received notice that a primary source of funding for our housing program was drying up. After a dozen years of significant and steady support, it was simply going away. It was a blow we felt deeply, but we had no idea that it was only the tip of the iceberg. Over the next month, support dropped like a meteor, and all without understandable explanation. In a catastrophic domino pattern, we watched as the financial foundation for the organization crumbled. We sat in the office and stared at each other in stunned disbelief and had conversations we never dreamed of having.

To complicate matters, in September Bruce fell ill and was the sickest I have known him to be since he was hospitalized with rheumatic fever at age eight. He was in bed for two weeks, which, for those who know him well, means he was close to death. When he finally turned the corner, he had lost twenty pounds and was haggard and gaunt. With a lot of uncertainty and trepidation, we navigated our way gently through the holiday season, making necessary adjustments but refusing to offer a dramatic, knee-jerk response to an intense situation. Patience and prayer were key.

As we entered 2020, we made more adjustments and had deep conversations about potential organizational decisions that would have to be made. Bruce met regularly with our Board of Directors and Executive Team to discuss the situation and absorb their insights and advice. The budget was evaluated and adjusted and additional funding possibilities discussed. We were loyal to our people but had to be fair and honest regarding the potential necessity of trimming the staff. In other words, we did all the practical things we knew to do and put forth our best efforts at stewardship. Still, we weren't sure about the future.

But none of this would have worked had we not made one all-important decision—we would renew our commitment to the mission, that is, the assignment Bruce had been given twenty-three years earlier. We would be obedient to it day by day and would leave the results to the one who had given the assignment. We would deepen our faith and be more open than ever in our proclamation that this is God's work, not ours. We would deep clean the City of Refuge culture and would only align ourselves with like-minded program partners and collaborators. We would not be drawn to the secular limelight, would not be motivated by the possibility of notoriety or financial success, and would not compromise the basic principles on which the ministry was originally built.

We would return to our roots.

Then came Covid. One would think that a pandemic would further draw the blinds on an operation that had experienced a major buckling of the knees only months before and had been struggling since. To be sure, City of Refuge dealt with the same challenges that rocked all institutions in our society—businesses, corporations, schools, churches, and healthcare systems—but as a housing facility, we could not completely shut down. We were classified as "essential" and continued to provide the basic services we are known for. Vocational training classes were suspended, traffic on campus was limited to essential staff and vendors, and programming for youth and kids was discontinued, but we were diligent in making the most of the situation. In essence, we returned to our roots of ministering to people in crisis and meeting basic needs, and doing so with a high level of confidence that God was going to sustain us along the way, and that he would make clear what our next steps should be.

And a strange thing happened—City of Refuge had its most productive year ever. New donors came on board and our financial situation not only stabilized but became stronger than it had ever been. To our amazement, income records were smashed in 2020 as mostly unsolicited funding showed up. Vocational training went virtual and our Workforce Innovation Hub placed nearly five hundred individuals into jobs, all during a pandemic. We learned, once again, that blessing follows obedience.

Today, City of Refuge is stronger in every area than it has ever been. We have a great team of professionals that operates with Passion and Excellence on a daily basis. We are well connected with program partners and collaborators. We have a strong, diverse, and influential Board of Directors. We are poised financially to expand our footprint exponentially in the coming months and years. We have fantastic City of Refuge Communities that are doing good works in their own towns and cities around the country. This is not happening because we are special or lucky or because we have manipulated things in our favor. It is happening because God chose a leader, gave him the tools to lead, assigned him a very important project, and entrusted him with it. And the leader said *yes* and continues to say *yes* every morning. In addition, others came along and discovered the opportunity to follow the leader, and many of us said *yes* and continue to say *yes* every morning. To be clear, many of us have leadership skills and exercise them in different areas of our lives, but when it comes to the vision and the work of City of Refuge, we follow.

On a good dog sled team, each member grows to understand his role and becomes comfortable with it. This makes for a smooth, efficient and productive journey. Lewis Grizzard said, "If you're not the lead dog, the view never changes." I get his point, but I don't think it should be about the view; rather, I think it should be about obedience to the role to which I've been assigned, knowing that reward awaits at the end of the journey.

Part 2

8

The Brawl

We make a living by what we get,
but we make a life by what we give.
—WINSTON CHURCHILL

....

IT WAS APRIL 6, 2019, and the University of Virginia men's basketball team was in the final four. If one is an avid UVA basketball fan, nothing could be more important, right? Wrong.

Bruce and I grew up on UVA basketball. We have always played sports and have actively followed college and professional athletics, but college basketball owns the top spot in our sporting world, and Virginia is king of that world. When we moved to the Charlottesville area at ages sixteen and fifteen, we found ourselves among a people group who oozed orange and blue and who could be heard screaming *Waaahooowaaahhh!!!* any time the Cavaliers took the court or field. We became serious fans, especially basketball fans, and guys named Walker, Iavaroni, Lamp, Sampson, Stokes, Jones, Alexander and Polynice became our sports heroes. UVA basketball was a big deal, and it still is.

In the early and mid-1980s, Virginia held the number one ranking in college basketball for more weeks than any other team in the country. On more than one occasion they entered the NCAA tournament as one of the favorites to win it all. But they never did. Even 7' 4" perennial All-American and three-time NCAA player-of-the-year, Ralph Sampson, could not lead his team to the promised land.

Year-in and year-out we maintained our loyalty to the Cavaliers, suffering through bad seasons, yawning through mediocre ones, and high-fiving each other when the team was good and sent Duke and North Carolina home whimpering. Several ACC regular season and tournament championships were obtained, but March Madness always brought disappointment. Nevertheless, we were Wahoos, in good times and bad.

In 2018, Coach Tony Bennett led an impressive squad to ACC regular season and tourney championships and took them into March Madness as the number one team in the country. The expectations were through the roof as they entered Round 1 against a community college from the suburbs of Baltimore, the number 63 team in the tournament and bottom seed in the bracket. When the buzzer sounded at the end of the game, Virginia had made history by being the first number one seed to lose to a bottom seed, an embarrassing and humiliating proposition altogether, and one that put us at the mercy of a passel of obnoxious UNC, Duke, and Virginia Tech fans for an entire year. It didn't help that the Cavs were trounced by twenty points.

Fortunately, the key players on the team decided to return for the 2018–2019 season for a shot at redemption, rather than declaring for the NBA draft. As the NCAA tournament began in March 2019, they once again found themselves in the top spot, having lost only three games all season, two of which were to a powerful Duke team that included future NBA lottery picks Zion Williamson and R. J. Barrett. Duke was favored to win it all but fell to Michigan State in the regional championship.

Virginia rolled fairly easily through the first three games, defeating Gardner Webb, Oklahoma, and a tough Oregon team. In the region finals, they overcame a barrage of three-pointers by Purdue point guard Carsen Edwards, hit a buzzer beater to tie the game at the end of regulation, and won in overtime in one of the best basketball games I've ever seen. The Cavaliers were in the Final Four for the first time since 1984.

On April 6, 2019, UVA would face one of the hottest teams in the country, the Auburn Tigers, in the national semi-finals, and it would be the second most important thing happening that evening.

*   *   *

Andrea hated men. In a brutal paradox that is repeated far too often in our society and around the world, she had been abused, abandoned, exploited, and damaged by men since her grandfather first started to molest her when she was five years old, but she believed that those same men were vital to her survival. Thus, she kept returning to them, because in her mind, it was better to belong to a clan that mistreats you than to have no clan at all. It's scary to be alone in the world.

In January of 2019, Andrea called 911 after having been beaten by her pimp, and she was taken to the emergency room to be treated for her injuries. When she exited the hospital, she began walking down the sidewalk and was offered a ride by a man who asked her if she wanted to party. Desperate for money, she told him yes and that the fee to party was thirty dollars. He smiled and pulled out a badge that identified him as an Atlanta police officer. Another officer opened her door and slapped handcuffs on her. She was arrested for prostitution and taken to Fulton County Jail.

A sympathetic judge who, in many cases, was known for offering long-term program opportunities in lieu of jail time, contacted the premier anti-trafficking rescue operation in the city and asked if they could find somewhere for Andrea to go. The next day she was delivered to House of Cherith, our residential program for survivors of trafficking and exploitation. Andrea was finally in a safe place, but her journey was just beginning. The severe trauma she had endured since she was a little girl had shattered her sense of self-worth, made her defensive and angry, and created a seemingly impenetrable wall between her and men. Although she was provided with a beautiful, clean, private bedroom at HOC, for the first two weeks she insisted on sleeping on the floor. Beds, no matter how beautifully appointed, were symbols of horrific experiences that stirred up terrible memories, and she wanted nothing to do with them. Residential Services personnel begged her to eat and struggled to get her to participate in activities or conversations with other residents. She only wanted to sleep or sit on the floor with a blank expression and rock back and forth.

When Bruce first saw Andrea in the corridor with the Intake Coordinator and introduced himself, she slinked to the wall and covered her face, refusing to even say hello. This became her pattern of behavior any time she encountered men who tried to interact. If there had ever been a shred of trust toward persons of the male gender, it had been buried under layers of betrayal and abuse. To peel off the layers would require a commitment to go to war on her behalf, thereby proving to her that there were men who would love her, provide for her, protect her, and prepare her for great things in the future, all without making demands or expecting anything in return. She needed to know that there are good men who will help just because they want to help.

Andrea is one of more than eight-hundred women who have discovered their pathway to healing at House of Cherith since its inception in 2013. The number increases daily. There is Samantha, who was trafficked for ten years, often confined in large animal crates in dank motel rooms. Today she works in a for-impact organization and advocates for women who have similar stories to her own. There is Tina, who was held in slavery by monsters who sold her to athletes and entertainers for nearly two decades. Today she is part of an agency that works to push legislation that protects victims and goes after traffickers and purchasers. There is Sonia, who found herself embedded in the sex entertainment industry because it paid enough to support her drug habit. She graduated from the HOC program and was hired as a member of the Residential Services team. The list goes on and on.

On that list is Anita, who grew up in extreme poverty and began selling her body at age thirteen to get food for her mother and younger brother. In the world of prostitution, she was introduced to drugs and became a hard-core crack addict. Her teen and young adult years were spent hustling to survive, and her addiction worsened. The years passed and her life fizzled away.

In her early forties, Anita reconnected with her daughter and grandchildren and found the strength to walk away from the drugs. She stayed sober for four years but was derailed when she got into a relationship with a man who led her back to the traps. She spiraled to the deepest levels of despair and hopelessness she had ever experienced. She was bouncing from hotel to hotel and drug house to drug house and robbing people to support her habit. Finally, after having left her daughter and two grandbabies to fend for themselves in an abandoned house, Anita hit rock bottom and cried out to God for help. As she prayed, the phrase *Out of Darkness* came to her mind, and she typed it into her phone and searched. It came up as an anti-trafficking organization in Atlanta that specializes in rescuing women who desire to leave the lifestyle and find a better way.

Anita made the call and team members from Out of Darkness picked her up and referred her to House of Cherith at City of Refuge. "I'll never forget that day," she says with emotion in her voice. "A girl named Ashley met me outside Door 21 and escorted me down the hallway. She was so nice. Everyone was so nice. We passed by a door on the back hallway, and she said, 'That's your house.' It didn't look like a house, but when we returned from the office and went through that door, man it was beautiful inside. It was a house, no, a home! Ashley took me to Room 6 and told me that was my room, and I couldn't believe it."

The commitment of the administrators, staff, and volunteers at House of Cherith is to Fight for Freedom for survivors who have rarely, or never, had anyone fight for them, but have always been pushed down and oppressed. Under the leadership of Executive Director Kelsi Franco, who is also Bruce's daughter, Fight Club was established a few years back to offer a structured way for supporters to be part of the fight every day. A few dollars a month helps to house, feed, clothe, and provide security to the survivor population. Fight Club members ensure that these precious ladies have a comfortable room and nutritious food, receive the therapeutic and recreational opportunities they deserve, as well as the counseling and trauma-informed-care they so desperately need. The commitments of Fight Club members save lives every day.

The power of collaboration, which leads to collective impact, has always been a lifeline for City of Refuge and its programs. In 2018, the emphasis on fighting for people who can't fight for themselves drew the attention of an organization called Brawl for a Cause, a group that supports nonprofit, or "for-impact," efforts by putting on boxing events in which representatives from the organizations fight to raise funds.

The early planning sessions for the 2019 Brawl included discussions around who would get in the ring to fight on behalf of the residents of House of Cherith. The previous year, Kelsi had battered a sweet girl from another organization, proving her commitment to fight for her ladies through blood, sweat, and tears. This time around, they were looking for someone to fight in the men's category, and it was apparent early on that Bruce would put no one in the ring except himself. He would draw the most attention. He would raise the most money. More importantly, as the father of five daughters, he was intense in his drive to protect and defend women and girls who needed to know that not all men are bad and that there are those who will put on the gloves on their behalf.

After months of training, fight night finally arrived—April 6, 2019. That's right, the event was scheduled the same night as the NCAA men's basketball national semi-finals, and the Virginia Cavaliers were playing. For the first time in my life, I saw Bruce move a hugely important UVA game down the priority list. All week leading up to the event, I talked about the possibility of the team we had followed for five decades bringing the championship trophy home, and Bruce talked about the fight.

Brawl for a Cause was held at the Georgia World Congress Center, and the atmosphere was giddy. I wouldn't have missed it for the world, but deep in the core of who I am, I was praying that there would be a television with the game on. UVA played the early game, and Bruce was late on the fight card, so it was possible to catch the game if a TV was available. It wasn't as good as sitting in my recliner with a cold drink and a big bowl of chips and salsa, but a man has to do what he has to do. As a last resort, I could have watched the game on my phone, but a big screen makes all the difference.

Thanks be to the Almighty, who I'm sure wears orange and blue, I arrived to find that the Congress Center's downstairs bar was open with the Final Four playing on the televisions. I was ecstatic until I realized that an Auburn watch party had assembled, and that the orange and blue I was surrounded by was not my own. To avoid being killed, or at best struck in the head with a corn cob, I decided to search for another spot. I discovered that a TV had been set up right outside the ballroom where the fights were taking place, so I set up camp to watch the game with a handful of other folks, almost all of whom were also fans of the wrong team.

In an instant basketball classic, Virginia built a double-digit lead late in the second half, only to see Auburn's sharpshooter get hot and make several three-pointers in a row to give them the lead as time ran down.

With the clock at 5.6 seconds, UVA down by two and in possession of the ball, Ty Jerome threw the inbounds pass deep into the corner to UVA's own sharpshooter, Kyle Guy. He pivoted and elevated, and with an Auburn defender closing in, lofted a three-pointer that came up short. The Auburn fans, both in the arena where the game was being played and in the building where I stood, exploded into celebration. The players on their bench danced like drunk people and waved their towels over their heads. The crowd behind the bench chanted *War Eagle, War Eagle!*

But wait, what was that sound? Was it a whistle? Why, yes, it was a whistle, and it would instantly flip the emotions of thousands of people upside down and turn their hopes and dreams in vastly different directions. Kyle Guy was fouled on the play and would go to the free throw line for three shots. His team trailed by two with half a second on the clock.

Kyle Guy, with the face of a fourteen-year-old, but the nerves of a hardened war veteran, walked to the line and sank all three foul shots as if he was in his backyard on a dirt court with a rim nailed to a tree trunk. Virginia would play for the national championship.

And it didn't really matter.

Fifteen minutes later and a hundred steps away, Bruce climbed into a 20' x 20' boxing ring to fight for the lives, health, happiness, protection, and opportunity for hundreds of women who had never had a man sacrifice anything for them. His whole life had prepared him for this moment.

Residents from House of Cherith, including Andrea and Anita, were in the audience and were visibly shaken, at times looking downright confused that this man would put on gloves and headgear and go to war on their behalf.

As ladies who had never known true love from a man stood screaming, cheering, clapping, and weeping, Bruce and his worthy opponent pounded on each other as if their own children's lives were at stake. In the second round, Bruce caught a sweeping right hook to the jaw and spun toward the ropes. He came down awkwardly on his left foot, and it was obvious that he could no longer put full pressure on it. He survived the round, but the referee would not allow the fight to continue. It was the first time I had ever seen him lose. But wait, perhaps it is possible to lose and win at the same time.

Months earlier, Bruce had been invited to speak at an event in California on the Monday night following The Brawl. At the time of the invitation, the Final Four was in the distant future, and the odds that UVA would be playing in the championship game were meager, so he accepted. Now he faced the prospect of missing his beloved Cavaliers as they played for the title. On Sunday afternoon, he boarded a plane for the West Coast.

By the time the plane landed, the foot that had been injured in the fight was terribly swollen, and Bruce could barely walk. He was soon being tended to by a doctor who informed him that the risk of blood clots was very high with such an injury, especially having been on a plane for five hours. The doctor ordered him to lie on his back with his leg propped up for the next twenty-four hours, and to only get up to go to the bathroom. Out with the speaking engagement, in with the national championship. Perhaps it was heaven's little reward. On Monday night, Virginia won its first national championship in a thrilling overtime game against Texas Tech. I danced hearty jigs and whooped and hollered like I'd won the lottery. I posted pictures of my UVA shirt and banner. Late into the night, Bruce, our little brother, Keith, and I texted back and forth with each other and fellow UVA fans. Redemption had been won and the celebration was on. But it really didn't matter. It was just basketball. It was just young men trying to put a leather ball through a steel cylinder. It was fun and exciting, but in the big picture of our human existence, it was enormously unimportant.

On Wednesday, Bruce was back at work, wearing the scars of battle in the form of bruises and a severe limp. As he approached his office in the back hallway, he saw Anita coming toward him, perhaps on her way to a class or a meeting with her Case Manager. She, like Andrea, had layers of suspicion and distrust toward men and was resistant to any interaction with them. Bruce expected the usual drop of the head, easing toward the wall to create distance, and silence, the usual behavior of a woman who has only known manip-ulation, abuse, and disrespect from men. Instead, her face lit up like the angel Gabriel had appeared in front of her, and she began to run straight toward the man who had proven in dramatic fashion that he cared.

"PASTOR BRUCE!" she screamed as she jumped into his arms, ignoring his injured foot and nearly knocking him to the floor. She burst into tears and repeated over and over, "YOU FOUGHT FOR ME! YOU FOUGHT FOR ME!"

Bruce had broken bones in his foot and lost the fight, but what a victory. He won the hearts and the trust of every broken woman who witnessed his willingness to risk his own health and safety to defend them and bring healing and restoration to their lives. If he had won the fight, the results would have been the same. If he had been knocked out by a haymaker with two seconds gone in the first round, the results would have been the same. The names of winners and losers on a scorecard notwithstanding, this was an eternal victory.

Anita does not know who her biological father is and has never known the satisfaction of having solid, loving relationships. Her experience at House of Cherith, including the stunning revelation that someone cared enough to fight for her, has motivated her to make good decisions and press forward. "I took the Brawl very personally," she says. "Everything changed for me that night. I'm part of a family!"

She graduated from HOC later that year, moved into her own apartment, and now works as a Residential Services Associate in the program and owns her own cleaning business. In her own words, "I'm in a good place!"

We still enjoy UVA basketball, but helping people get to "a good place" is much better than titles, trophies, or bragging rights.

9

Family

In the beginning God created the heavens and the earth.
The earth was without form, and void . . .
—GENESIS 1:1–2

....

VOID. THERE WAS NOTHING. God created the massive spectacle of the heavens and set under them a planet in consummate alignment with a sun that would give light and heat, a moon that would serve as a night-guide and would direct the tides of Earth's massive water bodies, and other planets in a spectacular universe. On that first day of creation, God performed work that no one else has ever been able to achieve—he made something from nothing, and the something was impressive.

But it was empty. *Void.*

Where there is emptiness, there is opportunity, even if the emptiness is shrouded in darkness. Dark emptiness calls for light so that everything that is right can be admired, and everything that is wrong can be evaluated and made right. When the light has completed its task of dispelling the darkness, the needs are made apparent, and the truth is revealed.

With his perfect plan in hand, the necessary power in his person to do the work, and the beautiful light he had pronounced over the dark void to illuminate what was right and what was wrong, God began to establish life on planet Earth. He created plants and trees, insects and every other creeping thing, wildlife and sea creatures, and birds and mysterious living things, some of which we have not yet identified. He looked out over his handiwork and knew that it was good.

But something was missing.

The creation of the heavens and the earth, along with the vegetation and animal life that were spoken into existence, was a magnificent accomplishment, but if the process had stopped there, it would have meant nothing and would have served no purpose except to demonstrate the power of the one who created it. If left there, the return to *void* was inevitable and would have happened in short order. The necessary addendum, to put it blandly, became the most impressive work that has ever been achieved—God created for himself a family.

Without family, the world doesn't work. As well, the world's most significant problems—poverty, war, crime and violence, injustice—are minimized at worst and eliminated at best, if brothers do not hate their brothers, and children do not despise their parents. I often say, "The order of God is the order of family." Family dysfunction, deterioration, and disintegration return us to the *void*, stealing from us everything that makes life full and free. Full, free life has always been God's intention for his family.

At the heart and soul of City of Refuge operations is a

goal to fill the empty spaces created by family brokenness. Programming for kids is offered to all who come our way, but for those who have been abused, neglected, abandoned, or orphaned, we seek to establish ourselves as the loving and protective family members that they deserve. We offer housing and wraparound services to women from every imaginable situation, but for those who deal with the absence of family support, or fallout from family trauma, or collateral damage from domestic violence, we offer ourselves as a community of brothers and sisters who can fill the gaps. Thankfully, hopelessness and defeat do not have to be the only possible end results.

In an ideal world, every child born would also be protected, provided for, and prepared for a productive life. It is no secret that we do not live in an ideal world, and the children are the ones who suffer most. The worldwide plague of producing children who are not protected, provided for, or prepared for the future is manufacturing destruction at levels that are indescribable. Compared to the apocalyptic course we are on, any pandemic that comes our way is dwarfed.

Bruce has five daughters—all beautiful and bright, and all born to parents who have loved, protected, provided for, and prepared them for whatever life brings, and who have done so consistently and obediently. But the Bruce and Rhonda Deel family has always been bigger than the seven of them. For the past nearly forty years, the family has added members like Jake, a former teaching pro at one of Atlanta's foremost country clubs, who became a homeless addict and alcoholic. For the last twenty years of his life, Jake knew without a doubt that he had a family that loved him and on whom he could depend. Although he never fully overcame his demons, when Jake was tired of struggling, he made his way back home, crawled into the back seat of Bruce's truck, and said goodbye to this world. He knew the family would take care of him.

Vanessa was a family member for twenty years as well. She was one of the first residents at the cold weather shelter we opened when the facility on Joseph Boone Boulevard was acquired in 2003. Vanessa had been on the streets for more than twenty years, selling her body to support a nasty drug addiction and hustling to survive. At twelve years of age, Vanessa's mother traded her to a man for a bottle of liquor. He began to abuse her, and she had her first child before she was thirteen. She began to self-medicate with drugs and alcohol and ended up in foster care. Her biological family had failed her, leaving a broken child to navigate a difficult pathway through life. As Mary Wollstonecraft said in the late 1700s, "A great proportion of the misery that wanders, in hideous forms around the world, is allowed to rise from the negligence of parents."[1] In that regard, not much has changed.

When she arrived at City of Refuge, Vanessa found a new family, and she wasn't about to go away. As Bruce says, "Some come to see. Others come for a season. Still others come to

---

1 Mary Wollstonecraft, *A Vindication of the Rights of Woman*
(New York: W.W. Norton & Company, 2009).

stay." Vanessa came to stay. Her lifestyle led to many physical challenges, some of which were irreversible. Two years ago, she suffered a massive stroke and became fully disabled. She spent months in the hospital, was moved to a rehabilitation center, and finished her time on earth under watchful eyes and in good care.

During the last few years of her life, Vanessa stopped telling the stories of neglect, betrayal, addiction, abuse, and so on. Rather, when she met strangers, she only wanted to talk about her City of Refuge family—Diddy (Bruce), Mama Rhonda, Unca Jeff, all her sisters, and the greater COR clan. On our last visit to the nursing home, she had trouble putting words together and was struggling to swallow a few bites of yogurt. She didn't recognize most people and wasn't always coherent, but there were two utterances she managed to spit out as soon as we walked through the door—"Diddy!" and "Unca Jeff!"

Oh, there was a third utterance that came in the form of a request—she asked us to smuggle in some snuff on our next visit! She went to her eternal rest before we could make another visit, but Bruce says he slipped a can of snuff into her coffin for the next life. He was kidding, of course.

Vanessa was born into void and chaos, but at City of Refuge she had the chance to step into the light. Illumination of what was right and what was wrong opened the door for physical, mental, and emotional healing while surrounded by a loving family. Hope began to rise, and her story started to change. Vanessa's transformation is illustrated in her journey from complete family brokenness to life as a valuable part of a loving family.

The results of parental irresponsibility, broken family relationships, lack of loyalty and respect inside the family unit, and abuse in any form can be crushing. Children who grow up as victims of the reckless behavior of injudicious adults suffer from low self-esteem, sexual confusion, unhealthy fear, behavioral issues, and the list goes on. Often, they turn to alcohol or drugs in an attempt to self-medicate, begin to experiment with illicit sexual behavior, or demonstrate a lack of respect for authority, which can lead to legal issues and a criminal record. The shattering of a proper family model leads to shattered lives.

Any expectation that government or social institutions, counseling or family restoration services, churches or other religious entities, or a thousand television talk show hosts can repair all the brokenness or fill the void that exists in so many families today will only lead to disappointment and frustration. God bless them all for what they do and for the results they achieve, but one cannot fill the Grand Canyon one bucket of sand at a time.

Although every honest effort at family healing and restoration is noble and to be cheered, it is a holy thing when solid, intact families make themselves available as vehicles of healing to those who have been damaged in the destruction of their own. If the devastation is too overwhelming, and there is no hope for their ghetto to become a garden, brothers and sisters, moms and dads, uncles, aunts, and cousins who have no biological connection can fill the void with love, provision, protection, and preparation for a bountiful future the empty vessel would never have known.

* * *

It was the summer of 1980, and Bruce and I were working at church camp in Roanoke, Virginia. Bruce was preparing to start his third year at Lee College, and I was one year behind him. Working summer camps landed us a few hundred bucks for school, not to mention we had a blast.

Of course, I do not recall the specific details of the moment it happened, but Bruce has a pretty good grasp on them. We were standing at the horseshoe pits, fulfilling our responsibilities as members of the recreation staff to manage the tournament and crown a worthy champion. We had won a record number of those tournaments ourselves. We were busy enforcing the rules, keeping score, and chasing shoes that seemed to still have the horse on them, when I saw Bruce staring up the hill as if he was in a trance. My eyes trained after his and landed on a young lady who was standing by a car and conversing with another camp worker.

What happened next requires speculation, but I imagine it went something like this:

"What're you looking at?"

"I'm looking at her. What do you think I'm looking at?"

"Well, I don't know why you're looking at her. What about Layne? Ain't y'all talking about getting married?"

"Nothing's official. I ain't marrying nobody 'til I find out who that is, and whether or not *she's* married."

"You're stupid."

That's a fair example of our communication styles back then, and sometimes even now. We have never seen the need to fluff our conversations and have never been thin-skinned when it comes to the abrasive opinions or blatant criticisms that may fly out of the mouth of the other brother. There is very little presumption in our relationship and almost no need for affirmation in either direction. We just tell the truth, or as near to it as we can muster in the moment. It works for us. We are also perfectly fine to ride in the same car for hours and not say a word.

The girl was Rhonda Ramsey, and in short order, she succeeded, whether intentionally or not, in busting up any wedding plans poor Layne may have been working on. Rhonda hailed from a preacher's family as well and grew up much like we did. She made it clear from the get-go that she did not want to marry a man who intended to serve in the ministry. She loved God and people, but the demands of pastoral life and the daily messiness of dealing with church people turned her off to the lifestyle. Besides, poverty was not something that fit into her dreams. It took seven years for Bruce to convince her that the right guy could turn the challenges into fascinating opportunities, and if done right, life in the ministry could be as exciting and rewarding as anything else, and maybe more. On Valentine's Day 1987, they were married.

In July of that same year, Rhonda calculated a plan to introduce me to a young lady from their church. The plan worked, and seven months later, Tracy and I were married. I am proud to say I beat Bruce to the punch when it came to being a father. The day I became Tracy's husband, I also became Dad to her two-year-old son. Ten months later, our first child together was born, followed by Bruce's first daughter later that year. Together we now have twelve kids— seven for me and five for him.

I have been told by several people, including my own mother, that we are crazy for having so many children. When I called to tell her number seven was on the way, her reply was, "Jeff, what's wrong with you?"

"What do you mean, Mom?"

"Do you know how much it costs to raise a child?"

"Yes ma'am, I have some experience."

"Well, the world is full of trouble, so why do you want to bring more children into it?"

Knowing my mom was a woman of deep faith, I decided to use Scripture on her. "Mom, you know the Bible says that children are a heritage from the Lord, and that the man whose quiver is full is a blessed man."

She thought for a moment, then responded, "Well, I just think it's time for you to have your quiver operated on."

That was the end of the conversation. I had no intention of diving deeper into that subject with my mother.

Rather than seeing our large families as burdensome, expensive, or potential victims of hard times in a cruel world, I see us as blessed to be able to bless. As I said, Bruce and Rhonda have added many biologically unrelated individuals to their family through the years, and those decisions have been easier and the quality of life made better for the people they embraced *because* of their large family, not in spite of it. Their girls have been sisters to orphans and have been there to help with the work and assist with the daily challenges of dealing with broken people. This big, tight-knit family has filled the void for so many with love, laughter, energy, compassion, and acceptance. At one point during their time of living in the church building on 14th Street, nineteen persons, besides the seven of them, lived there as well.

Through the years, Tracy and I have also been presented the opportunity to take in a few orphans and fill up some of the emptiness in their lives. We have done so under legal guardianship arrangements, and for one little boy who came our way, we facilitated an adoption to a young couple that could not have children. To watch our own kids work and sacrifice to make sure another kid has a better life is one of the most rewarding things I've ever experienced.

I tell these stories at the risk of sounding like I'm tooting our own horns or trying to gain some accolade. Nothing could be farther from the truth. I tell the stories and relate the information to offer a lesson on how a very satisfying life can be obtained. The philosophies of this world purport that we should get as much as we can for ourselves, strive to climb the ladder of success and become winners, and live at the top of the food chain. My experience has taught me that such an approach to life never leads to contentment. It never leads to satisfaction and peace. It only increases the hunger for more. It may result in more money, a bigger home, or a fancier lifestyle, but not contentment. Ironically, the pathway to satisfaction is paved with service and sacrifice. The more I obtain for myself, the emptier I become. The more of myself I choose to give away, the more abundant my life is.

A former orphan named Jeremiah adequately illustrates the beauty and power that can result when a loving family opens its doors and arms to a child born into brokenness. Jeremiah's mother, Guylene, grew up in Haiti and moved to France with her father when her parents divorced. As a young teen she witnessed the murder of her father by his own brother and subsequently transitioned to Miami to live with her mother. Her mother had remarried, and it wasn't long before the stepfather was sexually abusing Guylene and her sister. At seventeen years of age, the beautiful Haitian girl was pregnant.

The immediate demand was for Guylene to find an abortion clinic and have the pregnancy terminated. She found a clinic nearby and went for her appointment. As she lay on the table awaiting the procedure, a voice she thought belonged to her deceased father spoke and said, *Don't do it. Don't kill your baby.* She got up and ran from the clinic, terrified and confused. Twice more she was forced to go to the clinic, and twice more she heard the voice and ran from the room. On the third occasion, she was told she could not come back home if the abortion did not happen, so she gathered all the money she had saved and got on a bus to Atlanta.

Steve and Linda Grimes had made the move from traditional church to City of Refuge a few years earlier, and Steve had given up his career to come on staff. In February 2004, Steve was on his way to a staff meeting at COR when he received a call from his son, Matthew. Matthew expressed to his dad that he and his wife, Jenn, had decided to adopt a child. Jenn was unable to have children because of health challenges she had experienced when she was younger, but her heart's desire was to be a mother. Their desire together was to become Mom and Dad to a child without a family.

Guylene arrived at the Greyhound station in Atlanta knowing no one and without a plan, so she sat in the bus station for three days. On the third day, the security guard informed her that she could not live in the bus station and would have to leave. He told her about a nearby women's shelter and she walked the short distance and checked in. When she shared her story with a couple of other ladies at the shelter, they told her the place to go was to a church on 14th Street called Midtown Mission. The next day, she showed up.

At the meeting, Bruce announced to the team that a pregnant Haitian girl from Miami had arrived and had expressed her desire to put the baby up for adoption. Upon hearing her story, Bruce and Rhonda had immediately moved Guylene into the church building with their family and had begun to shower her with love and acceptance. She shared that she couldn't bear the thought of looking into her child's face every day and seeing the face of her abuser. She told them about the abortion clinic experiences and about her hopelessness in the bus station. She knew that her baby deserved to live but wasn't sure she could give him a good life, and she was tormented by the thought that he might look like the man who raped her.

Steve told Bruce about the call he had received from Matthew on his way to the meeting, and that Matt and Jenn had both had dreams that they would adopt a son, and he would be black. Bruce reluctantly informed him that another family had been waiting for an opportunity to adopt and was likely going to take the baby, but that Matt and Jenn would be on the list for future possibilities. Before sundown that evening, Bruce called to say that the arrangement with the other family had fallen through and to inquire if Matt and Jenn were still interested. The resounding answer was "Yes!"

On March 28, 2004, Guylene gave birth to a healthy baby boy and named him Jeremiah. Matt and Jenn and both sets of grandparents were there to welcome him into the world and into their family. Guylene was quiet and left the hospital the next day without completing the adoption paperwork. Unbeknownst to the Grimes family, she was being pressured by nurses and social workers to change her mind about giving her baby to a white family. She confided in Rhonda that she was confused and didn't know what to do. Rhonda told her that peace would come and she would know the right decision to make.

The next day, Rhonda returned from grocery shopping to find Guylene watching television in the living room. "Oh, Miss Rhonda," she exclaimed. "I was watching a lady Bible teacher on TV and she pointed at the screen and said, 'There is a seventeen or eighteen-year-old girl out there who is struggling with her decision about signing those papers. You need to go ahead and sign those papers and sign that little boy over.' Then she gave two verses from the book of Jeremiah. I know now what I must do!"

Note: I have been hyper-critical of television preachers for most of my adult life, but this time it worked.

Guylene signed the papers and Matt and Jenn became parents. Jeremiah is in his first semester of college and is the product of a loving, stable family environment. Because of the willingness of a young couple to become Mom and Dad to a child who was thrust into a world of chaos and emptiness through no choice of his own, Jeremiah has been loved, provided for, protected, and prepared for the future, as all children should be.

The Grimes family is just one of many in the COR clan that has given of their own lives to make the life of someone else better. April and Keith took in multiple foster children and eventually adopted two of them. Richard and Misty adopted two boys, one of whom was severely affected by fetal alcohol syndrome and was extremely difficult to handle. They stuck with it and today Marcus is a high school graduate, is maintaining his own residence, and working a full-time job. Paula, a single mother of two daughters, has been a foster parent to dozens of orphans and eventually adopted five of them, some with severe challenges.

I could fill an entire book (and maybe I will) with the stories of people who have chosen to become Mom, Dad, brother, sister, Unca, Auntie, or cuz to someone who has lived with a family void. Jim and Mary, Steve and Linda, Kyndal, Steven and Dawn, Tim and Sharon, Mandy, Kassi, Jonathan and Ashley, Gabe and Kelsi, Terry, Jeff and Ellie, Randy and Tina, Briggs and Katie, and the list goes on.

Families are filling the void.

As I'm writing this, I received a text message sent to the COR Leadership Team announcing a special event for kids in the City Kids daycare center tomorrow morning. It's called "Donuts with Dads." Many of the children who spend their days in the center are being raised by single mothers. Sadly, many of them have no relationship with their fathers, and a few of them have never met the man who participated in their conception. A dad-shaped void exists in their little hearts, but a call has gone out to men who may have never met these precious little ones, but who will be willing to show up tomorrow and do something a good dad will do. They will come with loving smiles and warm words, and will let the babies pick any donut they want. These are fathers with their own biological children, but they will take a few minutes out of their day to make sure fatherless children feel a little less fatherless.

Time after time we have seen the initial steps of spending time with and meeting practical needs of individuals who are experiencing the void and chaos of family brokenness lead to hope and healing. It's as if "Let there be light" is spoken again, and the revelation of what is right and what is wrong creates the opportunity for the good that exists to be praised, and for the void to be filled and chaos quelled. Inevitably, Light is followed by Hope, and the Hope increases dramatically when the person realizes she is not alone, but that there is a loving and supportive family in place to help fill the void. The beautiful resolution to the progression of Light and Hope is Transformation. It's the child who came to Eden Village with his mother, was enrolled in the City Kids educational program, and whose eyes were filled with trepidation, and whose emotions were unbalanced, but who now overflows with joy and exudes confidence, not to mention the academic growth of two grade levels at school. It's the young lady who saw herself only as a piece of property when she entered the City of Refuge gates, but who is now surrounded by sisters and brothers, father-figures and mother-figures, a big, beautiful family that is daily filling the void.

In the early days of doing programming for kids at City

of Refuge, a young fellow named Zavius Clemons became a mainstay. Zay, like dozens of other boys and girls in the program, was being raised by a single mother in an environment of poverty and lack of opportunity. His father was absent, and the male influencers in his life were typical to the culture and community into which he was born. Even his friends in the City of Refuge group looked to rappers, professional athletes, gang-bangers, and thugs in the community as their heroes. At City of Refuge, the boys found a new set of role models, and the contrasts were dramatic. Frankly, most of the boys who were active in the kids program with Zay went on to create their own criminal records, to develop lifestyles of hustling and irresponsible behavior, to father children they could not, or would not, take care of, and to transfer the cycle of poverty and chaos to the next generation. Zay, on the other hand, embedded himself in the City of Refuge family and became a true son of the house. He is now in his thirties and works as Facilities Manager on the COR campus. He calls Bruce "Pops" and their relationship is not much different than if he was a biological son. He is a great employee who is dedicated and loyal but is also present at the birthday parties, holiday gatherings, barbecues, and ball games hosted by the Deel family. As a side note, he is also a great father to his two daughters. Somewhere along the way, he learned how.

In the beginning, God created for himself a family, and his design was perfect, and his intentions have never changed.

10

Clothed
with Dignity

*What sort of world might it have been if Eve
had refused the serpent's offer and said to him instead,
"Let me not be like God. Let me be what
I was made to be—let me be a woman."*

—Elisabeth Elliot

FEW THINGS IN LIFE generate the range of human emotions that erupt when you give someone a car. The variety of reactions says it all. I have seen women gasp, cover their faces with their hands, and sob like babies. I have heard them scream and watched them dance like maniacs in the parking lot. Some have fallen to their knees and spoken in tongues; others have stood wide-eyed and trembling with their mouths hanging open. Inevitably, there will be lots of hugs and high-fives and many, many tears.

It happens when that teenager is called out to the driveway under the pretense that help is needed to carry in the groceries. She walks out grumbling, aggravated that her session on social media was interrupted, complaining that her younger brother is not called away from the video game he has been playing for hours, but that she has to be the one to do the work, again. But everything changes when she steps off the porch and sees a car she's never seen before, parked behind her mother's minivan, with a huge red ribbon plastered to the top of it. EVERYTHING changes. Her body's chemistry is instantly altered, resulting in an influx of joy, a volcanic eruption of positivity, and an explosion of love for everyone, even her little brother. A shiny symbol of her impending independence dominates the landscape before her, and life is suddenly very, very good.

If you are wondering why I would dedicate a chapter in this book to giving away cars, just hang on a minute. You may have never considered the medicinal qualities of a Nissan or the emotional support that exists inside the cabin of a Volkswagen. When you get into your ride and head out to wherever it is you are going, you may not have thought about how different your life would be if those four wheels were not under you, if you were walking, or riding a bike, or depending on public transportation, or forking out gobs of money for taxis or rideshare trips. If you've never considered how much a car enriches your life, you should. It might help to spend a few days with someone who needs a car but doesn't have one. The challenges are astronomical.

Consider Amber. She had done so many things right since making the life-saving decision to give House of Cherith a chance. She had committed herself to the steps in the process of addiction recovery, had been honest with her counselor and case manager, had exercised diligence as a student in the vocational training program, and had obeyed the rules. She graduated as a shining example to other residents of how to do the program the right way and was now making a livable wage at a good job. She had been reunited with her children, something naysayers had guaranteed would never happen, and was now functioning as a loving and responsible mother. Amber had made so much progress and was gaining confidence by the day, but inside she lived with a sense of restriction and hindrance, and she didn't really comprehend why.

At City of Refuge, creating environments and platforms for the perpetuation of self-worth is one of the most important things we do. Of our four core values—Passion, Excellence, Dignity, and Integrity, it is the gift of Dignity that feels the best and seems to have the most personal effect on the people we serve. Shame, humiliation, and low self-esteem characterize nearly every lady who comes to live at Eden Village or House of Cherith. If they ever had a sense of Dignity at all, it has been buried under layers of disappointment, rejection, fallout from bad relationships, or just plain bad luck. In many cases, Dignity is nowhere to be found. Its absence is sometimes manifested in their unwillingness or inability to look you in the eyes, tears that show up for no obvious reason, or an aversion to social interaction. At other times, loud obnoxiousness, bullying, and angry outbursts rule the day. All of the reactions are attempts at masking insecurities.

There is inherent beauty in empowering a person to feel good about herself. Compliments are okay if spoken in the right way but are easily misunderstood or can seem shallow and contrived. Rebuttal of self-criticism may be helpful for a moment, but the condemnation will return if circumstances do not change. Understanding this fact leads us to one of the keys to changing negative self-perception—change the circumstances! Prayer, counseling, verbal encouragement, group therapy, and lots of hugs are all valuable ingredients in the recipe for hope, healing, and confidence, but something else is needed. My gosh, let's give them new clothes and accessories, access to a fantastic beauty salon, a little makeup and a few pieces of jewelry, and, well, a car!

As it relates to providing practical assistance to people in crisis, nothing shaped my thinking more than a dark blip on America's history called Hurricane Katrina. In late August 2005, the Category 5 storm struck New Orleans and the entire region around it, taking 1392 lives and causing $125 billion in damage. It changed America's landscape, both literally and figuratively. Thousands of families evacuated, and it is estimated that approximately 100,000 individuals migrated to Atlanta. They arrived with bare essentials, and sometimes not even that.

In the aftermath of Katrina, City of Refuge became one of the largest collection and distribution centers for goods donated for victims of the storm. We had only been at the location on Joseph Boone for two years and most of the warehouse space was still empty. Large sections of the buildings quickly filled up with donated clothes, shoes, hygiene products, household goods, toys, bottled water, and many other items. We were able to assist thousands of people directly, and thousands more indirectly, through dozens of other agencies that came to us for loads of stuff.

Overwhelmingly, the most common item donated was used clothing. In times of disaster and crisis, people rush to their closets and dresser drawers, purging their wardrobes to help those in need. It is a two-way blessing—the donor gets rid of a lot of stuff they are not using, and the recipient gets stuff they need. We were happy to facilitate these processes, but the response was so overwhelming that we ended up shipping containers of donated goods to Haiti after the demand was satisfied.

It is absolutely appropriate to give away used clothing, shoes, and other necessities to those who have nothing, especially when sudden and unexpected disasters happen. However, in the methodical, daily process of rebuilding broken lives, there is something powerful about giving things that we would purchase for ourselves, giving things that are new with tags still hanging from them, giving things that are fashion current. Better yet, to allow ladies from which everything has been stolen, including their self-worth, to walk into a brightly lit and modern boutique to shop for themselves, to take their time and choose the items they really want, and to have to pay nothing at the counter, is transformational. To set appointments for them at a classy, modern beauty salon, and to allow them to choose their styles and colors, gives them a feeling of ownership over their own bodies and appearances, and establishes their importance among the general population.

These are the reasons we partner with Fab'rik, a designer clothing boutique, and Van Michael Salon, one of the most popular and trendy hair salons in Atlanta, to provide doses of Dignity to our ladies. Many of our residents arrive with everything they own in one or two garbage bags, and the items are inevitably old and dirty. You can be sure they do not want to change from the old and dirty things they have on to the old and dirty things that are in the bags, but it's all they have. When they are told they will be able to shop and pick out a few outfits, I'm sure their expectations are low. After all, the homeless are usually treated to the leftovers. But leftovers are not what they get here. They are escorted down the back hallway and arrive at a door with a sign that reads *Free Fab'rik*, and when they step through the door, let the party begin. Women have been known to fall to their knees in shock, squeal and jump up and down, burst into sobs and indiscernible groanings, and so on.

But the next thought is, *This is nice, but I ain't gonna look right in these new clothes with this jacked up hair and no makeup.* I have a wife and three daughters; I know how women think. That's when the ladies learn that the Van Michael Salon is right across the hall and their first appointment is set. Suddenly, you see a gleam in the eyes that wasn't there before. The chin starts to rise in confidence. The gait is no longer a labored drag from point A to point B, but a purposeful stride toward the next oasis or hurdle. Dignity begins to settle on them like a warm and well-fitting cloak.

* * *

It was Amber's turn. Dozens of times, City of Refuge and House of Cherith staff members had gathered on the parking lot near the NAPA Auto Shop and watched an unsuspecting resident or graduate stroll toward them on the arm of another staff person. I won't say they've been lied to, but they have been duped into believing they are being summoned to a meeting or some other decoy, but they are actually being set up for shock and awe. On this occasion, we had just finished a Night of Worship, and a large crowd of attendees was invited to walk to the shop for a little surprise. Everyone gathered around a 2008 white Mercedes that had recently been donated. Some knew what was happening, and some didn't. Amber was in the crowd of those who didn't know and was unwittingly poised to have much of the feeling of restriction and hindrance lifted from her shoulders.

A car is an inanimate, mechanical object without soul or spiritual substance, but it has the power to change a life. A car is a fortress against potential danger and a means to move through threats and obstacles. As a mobile shelter, it is highly symbolic and is capable of loosening the jaws of whatever trap a person is caught in. A car enables a person to escape the environment they are in and to move to the one they wish to be in.

Having a car is about having control of the things that are important to you. You can listen to the music *you* like. You can adjust the seat and temperature to your preferences. You can take your dog with you. A car is an extension of its owner, and the evidence is apparent everywhere, from the flavor of drink in the cupholder, to the fragrance of the air freshener, to the settings on the radio, to the announcements and statements displayed on bumper stickers. It is a rolling storage unit where you can keep your stuff under lock and key. It is a place where you can cry, curse, sing, pray, worship, and do so without fear of interference or judgment.

It is an absolute joy to witness the element of transformation that results from blessing someone with the gift of a vehicle. It is a move that dramatically increases their independence and autonomy. It gives them opportunities for financial security by expanding employment possibilities, and it grants to them a level of control that did not exist before over their own situations. Restriction and hindrance become freedom.

When Bruce pulled the title to the car and the keys from his pocket and called Amber's name, she rocked as if someone had bumped into her. It was a jolting physical reaction that reverberated through the throng of spectators. She doubled over and began to weep, as did many others in the room. It always happens. You see, it's not just about the car, or the beauty treatments, or the fashion. It's about a boost in self-worth and confidence. It's about breaking barriers and building momentum. It's about a mom being able to buckle her kids into the back seat of her own car and head off to take care of her business. It's about Dignity.

11

Pray, Wait,
Get Up and Move

The greater the obstacle,
the more glory in overcoming it.
—MOLIERE

....

A CHILD'S MIND is a fragile thing and is deserving of careful cultivation and tender guidance. Children, whether by design or default, depend on the adults in their lives to tell them the truth, to model responsibility and morality, and to prepare them for the future. Adults who bring children into the world are tasked with the most important job given to any human being—to protect their kids from physical, mental, and emotional harm, and to instill in them solid values that will sustain them through life.

In Danyale's case, the adults in her life failed in their most important responsibility. Danyale was born in Chicago in the late eighties to a teen mother and came home to poverty, dysfunction, and addiction. Unfortunately, it is a story we have come to be very familiar with, a story that is commonplace in our society, a story that has been repeated over and over at City of Refuge. The stories have different names, faces, and details, but they all go back to the irresponsibility of adults who produce children that they cannot or will not care for properly. In many cases, the children are rescued by loving grandparents who step in to fill the parental role, an act which is admirable but unjust. In Danyale's case, the grandmother struggled with alcoholism and a gambling addiction, traits she had inherited from the generation before her. There was no safety net, so the child was in a perpetual state of unsettledness, bouncing around to any relative or friend who would keep her for a few days, often left alone and hungry and faced with the horrors of mental, emotional, and sexual abuse at a very young age. When she was six years old, Danyale went to live with the mother of her mother's boyfriend (confusing, I know), where she enjoyed the most stability she had ever known, but it only lasted a year and she was shipped to Mississippi to live with a relative.

Danyale enjoyed life on the farm in Mississippi, tending to animals and picking berries and enjoying the outdoors, but it, too, was short-lived. The family she was living with was tired of the burden and expense of raising another child, and the little girl soon found herself back with her mother. Her circumstances worsened as her mother had become more heavily addicted to drugs and was showing signs of severe mental illness. Once again, the child was bounced around like an unwanted dog, often left for days in the dirty and drug-infested homes of total strangers, and often mistreated in despicable ways.

A tear traces down Danyale's cheek as she says to me, "At that time, I didn't understand abuse. I didn't know what was going on. I thought it was normal. I didn't understand what abandonment was, but I felt it. Now, I understand it."

She was just a child.

At seventeen years of age, with the mountainous burden of adulthood and self-sufficiency on her shoulders, Danyale came to Georgia to see if she could find anything worth living for. Her mother's addiction had completely robbed her of the ability to think rationally or behave responsibly, so the young girl had to figure out if she could make it on her own. She was void of self-esteem and confidence and had dropped out of school. The barriers were monumental. The need for companionship and financial support led to a relationship that started well but soured over time. Once again, she was stuck. Income from her job at a fast food restaurant was helpful but kept her in a perpetual state of poverty. She flipped burgers for eight years in Acworth, Georgia, because it was all she could do.

Because of a pandemic that put the world on pause and took millions of lives, 2020 was a year that will forever live in infamy. For Danyale, it was a pandemic and then some. As bad as her past had been, it had only foreshadowed the darkness and hardship that came in that dreadful year. In a span of a few months, she had lost her job, been abandoned by the person who helped keep a roof over her head, resulting in homelessness, and had been locked out of the Department of Labor website and her opportunity to draw unemployment benefits. She sank into major depression and resorted to reclusiveness in whatever dark room she could find. Hope became even more deeply buried under the rubble of two decades of destruction.

One of my favorite verses in the Bible is Psalm 12:5 in *The Message* translation, and it speaks perfectly to Danyale's situation:

Into the hovels of the poor,
Into the dark streets where the homeless groan, God speaks:
"I've had enough; I'm on my way
To heal the ache in the heart of the wretched."

In her homeless groaning, Danyale tells me that she was inspired to do three things: pray, wait, and get up and move. She began to pray and ask God to show her where to go. She waited until an idea came—get on a bus and go to Atlanta. Without knowing that a place like City of Refuge even existed, she got up and moved. She arrived in the city without a place to lay her head, so she prayed again and waited. She located a friend who lives in our neighborhood, and the friend told her to send an email to Crossroads, a ministry that provides practical assistance to homeless people. The response from Crossroads informed her that an organization called City of Refuge was right around the corner and that a referral had been made.

In her own words, "It was the place that would change my life forever."

The wounded child who had known nothing in life but poverty, abuse, abandonment, and pain, entered the gates at City of Refuge laden with fear, timidity, and skepticism, but she was immediately greeted by people who treated her like family. When telling her story, Danyale emphasizes that the very thing that failed her as a child and young woman has now become a lifeline and a vehicle for success. The professionals in our housing program, who welcomed her on campus assessed her situation, formulated an individualized plan, and aligned her with the right services and programs, also loved and befriended her and treated her like a sister.

The genuine care she received from these professionals, including her case manager, Vallise Rudolph, was paramount to breaking down barriers and building momentum. She now had a good family. The words came back: *pray, wait, get up and move.* She had prayed and waited, now was the time to move. And move she did.

In four months, Danyale earned her GED from Atlanta Technical College and, one month later, enrolled in regular classes to pursue a degree in Science and Nursing. She is in her third semester of an accelerated program and is carrying a 3.3 GPA. A year ago, she attended a UPS job fair in our Workforce Innovation Hub, was hired immediately, and is still working the evening shift. She has goals to be a traveling healthcare professional, to help others who are living in cycles of generational poverty and abuse, and eventually to own her own home.

Danyale wants to extend her blessings to others, assisting with educational pursuits, financial stability, and restoration of broken family relationships.

The cycle has been broken.

Danyale is one person, but she is representative of humanity at large and of so many people we have encountered at City of Refuge through the years. She recently subscribed to Ancestry DNA and discovered that she is a mixture of British, Latino, and West African heritage. She is, literally, a blend of the world's peoples. In her own words, "I'm on a mission to know myself," and it's a beautiful mission. She is not content to live inside the box that others built for her, nor to identify with and embrace the cycles that controlled the lives of her ancestors.

One of the powerful exclamations to her story is that Danyale now stands as an example to other women who come through the gate fearful and skeptical. No matter how bad life's experiences have been or how tall and thick the resulting barriers, we can point to Danyale and say, "Let me tell you about her."

12

Indispensable

There comes a time in your life
when you have to choose to turn the page,
write another book or simply close it.
—SHANNON ALDER

....

MY FOURTH GRANDCHILD, Ellis Andrew Kelly, was born yesterday. He is a 9 lb., 7 oz. beautiful, chunky bundle of sweetness. On his first day on planet Earth, I held him for more than an hour. We had a fabulous, albeit one-sided, conversation, and I told him that he is a treasure and that he will always be valued, loved, and protected. I thought about his innocence, helplessness, and vulnerability, and how he will depend totally on others for everything he needs for the first few years of his life. I thought about everything he will need to learn to be successful, and how he will depend on the adults in his life to recognize his bents and guide him toward his God-given purpose. A famous proverb says, "Train up a child in the way he should go, and when he is old he will not depart from it" (Proverbs 22:6). The prepositional phrase "in the way he should go," indicates a responsibility that begins with recognition of aptitude, talent, and giftings, and an intentional plan to promote, support, encourage, facilitate, and affirm the child as he grows and goes. The instruction includes elements of protection, nurturing, and responsibility, along with a heavy emphasis on the role of parents and other adults involved in the raising of children, to prepare them for life, and to do so according to their individual bents.

I thought about the world Ellis will grow up in and how vastly important it is for him to be told the truth and gently guided along the right pathway. He will need sound instruction, stable guidance, and grounded role models. He will need protection from deception and instruction on how to find balance. He will need a lot of love and provision. Ellis cannot provide these things for himself; they must come from the people who have been charged with the responsibility for his life.

Seven days before Ellis was born, I sat with two of the finest employees our organization has on its roster. As I sat with them and listened to their stories, I silently gave thanks that they are still alive and able to share very difficult details about where they came from and what they have overcome, or are still overcoming. Holly and Katherine are both graduates of House of Cherith and are stepsisters. Holly's father is married to Katherine's mother.

You may or may not believe in miracles, but it will be impossible for you to review the narrative of the lives of these beautiful young women, to see where they are today, and to not conclude that their stories of transformation are being written by a supernatural entity that is more capable and powerful than they are or could ever become. As I reflect on the conversation I had with them, I can't help but wonder what the first day of their lives was like. Were they held and caressed by a loving grandfather? Did someone gush adjectives about their eyes, cheeks, or hair? Did their little ears hear sentimental whispers from people who valued them more than their own lives? Did they lie on the rising and falling breast of the mothers who had just endured the most intense pain known to humans in order that they might have a chance to live and grow? Did they hear her say how much she loved them?

Holly entered the world in the same fashion as Ellis and the rest of us. I'm not sure what her first day, or week, or month consisted of, but I do know she was introduced to chaos not long after arrival. In Holly's world, addiction was simply a way of life, and the lack of order that resulted from it was normal to her. Her father sold and used drugs and was a monster in the home, abusing Holly and her biological sister in horrific ways. Addiction gripped her mother as well, and the girls were left unguarded and vulnerable. Finally, when Holly was twelve, her father was sent to prison and the abuse stopped, but the damage was done. Raised without boundaries and searching for love and acceptance, she became sexually active and was pregnant by age fourteen.

Holly married the father of her child, but the marriage was short-lived and she would soon be a divorced sixteen-year-old mother. In an unexplainable phenomenon that has been repeated countless times, the next man she married was just like her father. She got pregnant again, but the physical abuse caused a miscarriage. A third pregnancy resulted in the birth of a daughter, but the violence continued and became more intense. Holly was often beaten, shoved to the floor, and terrified as her husband pressed a gun to her head. He seemed to enjoy kicking her in the back, leaving bruises in the shape of his boot and causing her to suffer chronic back pain. Her life was a nightmare. Her father was in prison and had proven he could not be counted on for any of the invaluable elements of life that children should be able to look to their fathers for, and her mother offered little support.

Another son was born, and the abuse intensified even more, but threats to take her children and never let her see them again were enough to make her stay; that is, until Holly discovered that the "accidents" that were perpetually sending her oldest son to the emergency room were really the results of physical abuse by her husband. She left with the child, but the younger two stayed behind. To numb her pain and alter the reality of the situation, Holly began to abuse pain medication and was soon in the throes of hardcore opioid addiction. Her husband manipulated her into moving back in with him and they sank deeper and deeper into a nearly identical lifestyle to that in which she had grown up. The violent attacks ramped up and she was soon homeless and completely destitute.

In a healthy family environment, the family member who is in trouble is able to first look to blood relatives for support, security, and stability. Most especially, a child, no matter what age, should always be able to turn to her mother for these things. Holly tried, but her mom was bound by her own addiction and had inherited the ability, or had learned from experience, how to be abusive and manipulative in her own way. She received her daughter and grandkids with open arms, pledging to provide a haven for them, offering the bounty of grandmotherly love and support she had to offer, but soon wearied of the challenges and became another source of rejection and pressure. At a point of absolute helplessness and desperation, Holly turned her children over to her mother-in-law, and by default, fell into the category of homeless drug addict, doing what she had to do to survive, but praying every day that God would decide to take her out of this world.

Tears well up in Holly's eyes as she describes the brokenness that characterizes every aspect of family life she has ever experienced. Her life as a daughter, sister, and mother has been the antithesis to God's design. It is a fractured and chaotic picture of what happens when children are produced but not protected, not provided for, not prepared for the future. But there is light at the end of her dark tunnel, and each day she is seeing that light expand and illuminate the good that awaits.

The lives of Holly and Katherine collided when they were in their mid-teens. While her father was in prison, Holly's parents had divorced, and after his release her dad met and married another woman, a woman who brought into the family a daughter who, because she was the only biracial person in the family, was already struggling with issues of self-worth and acceptance. Katherine was a smart, beautiful young lady but now found herself under the government of a racist redneck who hated her. The prejudice was palpable in the home, and in a scenario scarily similar to that of Holly, Katherine's mother was either powerless or unwilling to protect her daughter from the monster.

Katherine began to take pills to alter her mental state and help her cope with the situation. Self-medicating seemed the only viable option in a world where there appeared to be no healthy alternatives to the hell in which she was living. She followed the pattern of so many young women who are void of the love and affection they should receive from their fathers, and at sixteen she was pregnant. She was unwittingly mirroring the life of her stepsister. Bringing a baby into the home only increased her stepdad's animosity and the pressure intensified. When she was eighteen, Katherine took her toddler and moved in with her grandfather. She turned more and more to drugs in order to cope and began to work as a petty dealer to support her own habit.

Life in the new location was more of the same, and Katherine sank deeper and deeper into a pit of addiction and destitution. She lived, off and on, with her grandfather but was victimized by other relatives and never settled into a comfortable and normal way of living. A couple of years passed and the darkness that shrouded her life intensified, but finally good news arrived—her "real Dad" wanted to meet her. Katherine had always wanted to know her biological father. Perhaps he would be her knight in shining armor. Perhaps he would begin to protect her and help create positive opportunities for the future. Perhaps he would simply do what fathers are supposed to do.

But he wasn't the hero she had always hoped for. He didn't bring hope, healing, and protection to his broken daughter. He was just next in the long line of bums who added to the gathering tsunami of destruction that was washing over her life. "On the first night after we met," she says with difficulty as tears stream down her face, "he packed a meth bowl and we smoked it together." Rather than protecting her, he put her in the company of other bums who began to use her as a peon in their petty illegal drug operations, giving her enough heroin to satisfy her own cravings, and requiring her to sell drugs for them as payment. She reconnected with the father of her child, a move which amounted to having another partner with whom to share a needle or pipe. A daily lifestyle of using and dealing led to legal problems and they both landed in jail.

For Katherine, the next few years were like living inside a cyclone, void of any sense of order or meaning, tossed here and there without purpose, fully expecting at any moment to be annihilated and forgotten. She cycled in and out of homelessness, jail and abusive relationships. Despite battling kidney issues from years of drug abuse, she got pregnant again and the need for pain pills was more prevalent than ever. When the pills ran out, she ran for something else, anything that would bring temporary relief. She obtained an apartment but went back to jail on a probation violation, only to find an eviction notice from her landlord upon release. Once again, she was homeless and was living in her car, using any drug she could get her hands on, " . . . just to not feel."

Whether it's the proverbial end-of-the-rope, bottom-of-the-barrel, or some other adage, there comes a point in the life of a person who has been robbed of opportunity and given over to the clutches of addiction and depression, when they run out of hope. That moment came for Katherine after four months in her car, doing nothing but getting high, crashing, screaming, trembling, and doing whatever was necessary to get the next fix. She finally got her hands on enough dope to kill her, and she willingly put it into her body, relieved in a deeply tragic way that the nightmare was about to end. Hope that a better day would arrive finally petered out. Hope that someone, anyone, would show up to take her by the hand and lead her to a better place finally trickled like sand falling from an hourglass, until there was nothing but emptiness.

* * *

Holly had lost her children and was under the complete control of her addiction. Any hope for something better was ebbing away and she scrambled for any thought or idea that might

ABOVE:
Deel homestead,
West Virginia,
early 1950s

LEFT:
Cecil and
Dawn Deel's
wedding day,
June 6, 1958

Bruce's first birthday, August 10, 1961

Colorado, 1961

The early years, Suffolk, Virginia, 1963

Family of five, 1971

Bruce and Jeff, 1974

Family of six, 1976

The polyester days

The Reverend Cecil Deel

Grandma and Grandpa Landreth

Our home, mid 70s

Dad, Indian Valley, Virginia

City of Refuge begins at The Mission, 1997

TOP: Aerial View of COR, 2023   ABOVE: A family on a journey

Auto tech training

Auto tech graduation

TOP:
Culinary graduation

ABOVE: City Kids
preschoolers

LEFT: City Kids
preschool graduation

TOP: City Youth working on bikes
ABOVE: City Youth at the COR farm

ABOVE: Summer event with City Kids

LEFT: Bruce in a dunking booth at a COR event

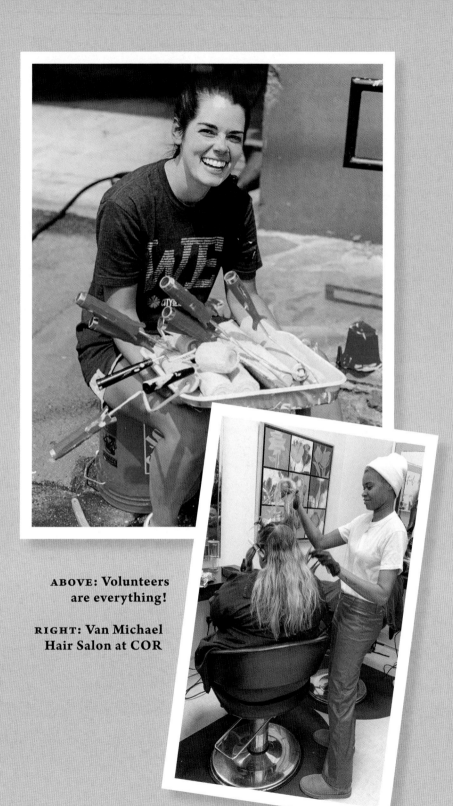

ABOVE: Volunteers
are everything!

RIGHT: Van Michael
Hair Salon at COR

TOP: Welcome Home women's transitional house
ABOVE: The 345 men's center

Bruce Hodge, Greg Washington, Willie Jackson
("The Bones Are Good" Lifers)

Bruce speaking at the 2023 annual gathering

Jeff

cause the smallest ray of light to appear on her dark pathway. She found out her sister was coming from California for a visit, and Holly knew she must find a way to connect with her sister and ask for help. Though living in chronic homelessness, she would bounce in and out of her mother's house to shower and grab food, but always knowing the visits must be quick to avoid a blow up. She needed access to a phone that had her sister's number in it, and her mom's phone was all she could think of. She formulated a plan to steal the phone during one of her desperation visits, and the plan worked.

"Come rescue me," Holly said when her sister answered the phone. "I'm in trouble, please come rescue me."

Holly sits in the chair across from me, and I can hardly believe the same young lady who throws her head back and laughs, rolls her eyes at certain points in the conversation as if the whole thing is ridiculous, and reaches over to comfort her stepsister with a light touch on the arm, actually lived through the things she just described. I often see her driving one of the House of Cherith transport vehicles on and off campus, always smiling as she takes current residents for appointments, goes grocery shopping for one of the houses, or completes some other task from her daily checklist. She is happy and healthy—fully alive, one might say. Like a solitary cloud on a sunny day, there is a sadness that passes over her eyes when the subject of her children comes up. The younger two are still with her ex-husband's mother, and to regain custody would involve a long and expensive legal battle. "I'm not ready for it yet," she says through tears. "One day I will be, maybe, but not yet. I've still gotta work on myself; my kids are in God's hands."

In her search for an option for Holly, her sister happened to meet a lady who is part of the City of Refuge family. Her sister shared Holly's story with the lady, and the immediate response was an offer to help. They went for Holly and brought her to a COR campus in their community, where she went through the excruciating process of detoxification, followed by an eight-week stay at the Penfield addiction recovery program for women. Given no window for fault or failure, she was taken directly from Penfield to House of Cherith where she spent two and a half years working through her individualized case plan. With the help of counselors, trauma-informed-care specialists, instructors, and residential services associates, she plowed through the mountains of emotional and mental rubble that had been created through the years. By her own admission, she still has some work to do, but, "I ain't where I used to be," she says with a smile and a roll of the eyes.

After graduation from HOC, Holly was hired to work for the organization and was approved for a brand-new apartment in a permanent supportive housing complex. She has been an employee at HOC for three years and is gaining valuable experience working with women in crisis, but she won't be there forever. Her goal is to become a social worker specializing in working with domestic violence survivors.

The pain of being separated from her younger children

is somewhat buffered by the relationship Holly has with her oldest son. "We have a great relationship," she says. "You know, we kinda grew up together!" She beams with pride as she speaks of him, and an unspoken, but obvious, relief settles on her countenance, relief in knowing that he did not settle for the vicious cycle in which he grew up. He is twenty-two now and has been in the U.S. Army for four years.

Holly is also finding fulfillment and satisfaction in rebuilding the relationship with her mother. Much grace and forgiveness are required from both sides, but apologies have been issued and progress is being made. Hope once seemed dead, but it rises from the ashes a little more each day and is slowly putting on muscle.

"Everything is in God's hands," she declares, "and I'm going to make it."

* * *

The scenario was likely something like this: "Call nine-one-one! There's a girl passed out in this car. She may be dead."

But she wasn't dead. Katherine didn't ask to be saved, and didn't want to be saved, but she had been found in time and was rushed to the hospital where she received the treatment necessary to counteract the drugs that were in her system, and her life was spared. She was charged, again, with possession of illegal substances and went to jail for a year. The time behind bars was a blessing as she was shielded from the destructive implements that characterized her life on the outside, and she was afforded time to think about and process all that had happened through the years and to assess whether or not there was a chance for redemption.

It was during her last few weeks of incarceration that family members began to tell her about her stepsister's progress at a program in Atlanta. They encouraged her to consider it, and she did. She was ready for change. It might work, and it might not, but anything was better than what she had experienced so far.

Katherine was out of jail two days before moving into House of Cherith and beginning her own journey to healing. With her stepsister right there as an example of the possibilities, she dove headlong into the program and graduated in two years as a model resident and student. She was hired as a teacher in the City Kids daycare center on campus and is living independently in her own apartment. She was tapped by Furnish with Love, another nonprofit organization in the city, to receive all new furnishings and amenities for her residence, the last requirement for regaining custody of her kids, ages seventeen, five, and four. On St. Patrick's Day 2023, the project was completed and Katherine's family took a giant leap toward restoration.

*　*　*

My grandson, Ellis, is now a few days old and is keeping our joy buckets full. I held him again yesterday and his beautiful brownish-grayish eyes wandered across my face with seeming attempts to focus, but wandering nonetheless. It occurs to me that Ellis, Holly and her kids, Katherine and her kids, all the adults in their lives, and all the adults and children in all of our lives, have the same value. We are, each one of us, created in the image of God and have been placed on Earth to reflect that image wherever we go. In God's eyes, there are no more-thans and less-thans, important people and unimportant people, valuable folks and throwaways. He does not categorize his children by physical appearance, intelligence quotient, talents and abilities, financial status, or the number of "friends" we have on our social media accounts. He does not look with favor and pleasure at the handsome and successful businessman, who buzzes from his stylish home in a gated suburban community to a posh office in the city, while frowning with disdain at the smelly beggar who panders for beer money on the street corner. The two men are equal in the eyes of the one who made them, and the circumstances of their individual lives do not dictate or diminish their value. We are not like produce at the market that is reduced if it has been dropped, bruised, or is out of date.

Our individual reflections of the Creator can certainly be tarnished by lifestyles that contain characteristics not of his nature, but his love is not diminished. Holly and Katherine were victims from the day they were born, but each of them was afforded the opportunity to move from the category of victim to the category of survivor, and ultimately to the category of overcomer. They seized that opportunity.

I was in the room a few years ago when the announcement was made to the residents of House of Cherith that Terri, another beautiful young woman from the same North Georgia community as Holly and Katherine, had died from a drug overdose after leaving the program. I was sitting across the room from Holly and will never forget her reaction. The news almost knocked her out of her chair, as if she had been struck with a heavy object. An involuntary shriek exited her lungs and she crumpled into a sobbing heap. She loved Terri—they were friends, but I sense there was more to it than just the devastating loss of such a precious and potential-filled life. Holly understood how easily the announcement could have been about her, about Katherine, about so many of the ladies who sat with her in that room.

Baby Ellis, Holly, Katherine, and Terri make up a collage of humanity, and each one is to be viewed as indispensable, no matter their number of days or what those days have consisted of. We lost Terri, but we learned lessons from her life and gained value by knowing her. We believe she is wrapped in her Creator's arms, and she is still indispensable. Holly and Katherine have done many things they are not proud of, many things they are ashamed of, but they are overcoming day by day, and they are indispensable. And Baby Ellis, well . . .

13

Success
Looks Like . . .

We must accept finite disappointment
but never lose infinite hope.
—MARTIN LUTHER KING, JR.

....

AT CITY OF REFUGE and House of Cherith there
will be days, sometimes weeks, of disappointment
as those we care for fail to fully embrace all we offer
and continue to live in their places of pain and
disappointment. That cruel fact is something we
must accept. But, while understanding that disappointment will come, we must commit to never
lose infinite hope. We have to cultivate hope that
is eternal, that is infinite, that never ceases. We are
doing the right work and we are doing it the right
way. That's all that is required of us. Everything else
is up to God, and our hope should always be firmly
planted in him and his perfect ways.

—BRUCE

In my estimation, there is nothing of greater value that the children of Cecil and Dawn Deel possess than the understanding that it is a monumental mistake to judge someone if you don't know their story. Many times, our inclination as humans is to pass judgment and draw conclusions regarding others based on behavior without consideration for why the behavior exists. In other words, we judge based on *what* they do rather than *why* they do it, and we tend to view their behavior through the lens of our own experience rather than through the lens of what we have learned about theirs. We pass a homeless person begging for coins on the street corner and think to ourselves, or sometimes even say aloud, *Why doesn't he just get a job?*

There is a characteristic of brain function called cognitive bias that causes us to rationalize based on our personal experiences or preferences. It serves as a mental default filter that is constructed by what we've been taught, what we've been through, or what we would personally prefer. In other words, our brains are pre-wired to think a certain way or to interpret a situation. For example, if a person is attacked, beaten, and robbed by someone of a different race, a cognitive bias may develop that causes the victim to think negatively about all people of the other race. Thus, a singular traumatic incident results in an overall unwarranted racist attitude. A child who grows up in meager circumstances and is at some point treated poorly by a wealthy person may draw the conclusion that all wealthy people are snobby or cruel. A cognitive bias has been created that, unless extracted, will cause negativity toward an entire category of people to always be there.

For "ordinary" people, whose minds are well-developed and healthy, who have not suffered debilitating trauma, and who are not slaves to addiction, *Why doesn't he just get a job?* may be a fair question. Unfortunately, a significant percentage of homeless people are not well—mentally, physically, or both. Statistics from an organization that works with homeless people in Cincinnati show that 58 percent of the people who walk through their doors and receive an assessment are struggling with mental illness that is significant enough to prevent them from living normally without medication. The fact notwithstanding that there are legitimately lazy people in every city and town, we should not forget that the list of symptoms of laziness is nearly identical to the list of symptoms of depression.

There is a way to disassemble the filters in our brains that cause us to draw uninformed conclusions or to rush to judgment based on a person's behavior, and it starts with getting to know their story. Our parents taught us to love and accept people, especially broken people, and they demonstrated that to really love them, you have to really know them. I may feel empathy or compassion, but to really love them requires that I get mixed up in their lives and hear their stories. At times, this kind of approach can be quite messy because climbing into the ditch with folks who have been robbed and beaten and left for dead, like the man encountered by the Good

Samaritan, will always be messy. Regardless of the blood, tears, snot, or inconvenience involved, it is our responsibility as human beings to climb into that ditch to find out why they're there and to see if we can help. Likewise, it is our responsibility, to the extent that they will allow it, to help them out of the ditch and to take them down the road to discover their pathway to healing. It is tragic to think of the number of people who have languished in the ditch because those who could have helped allowed a cognitive bias to steer them to the other side of the road.

Sometimes we are asked how effective our efforts are. "What percentage of the people who you try to help actually overcome their problems and become stable, productive citizens?" It's a common question. Or, "What is your success rate?" Or, "What does success look like for the people you serve?"

The answer is that we don't know, but what we do know is that a more complete answer depends on how success is defined in a given situation. Let me see if I can use one example to explain.

Success for Jennifer Johnson is that she died at thirty-two years of age. The hell that comprised her life was finally over. Jennifer's destruction began when she was born and was brought home to addiction, chaos, and dysfunction. Her parents prioritized drinking, getting high, and entertaining guests with long criminal records over taking care of the brand-new baby girl they had produced. When Jennifer was five, her twelve-year-old brother found pornographic material left in plain view by irresponsible adults, and began to invite friends from the neighborhood over to watch the videos. Led by her own brother, the boys seized the opportunity to act on what they had seen in the videos and to use Jennifer as their object. The parents were oblivious, or didn't care.

The sexual abuse, along with neglect and emotional trauma, continued throughout the little girl's childhood and adolescent years. During her early teens, she began to consume alcohol and smoke marijuana with boys in the trailer park where she lived. She was taken out of her home and placed in the foster system, but the problems continued until her life was completely immersed in addiction, violence, sexual promiscuity, and run-ins with police. She bounced from home to home and was a perpetual threat to run away. At nineteen, she aged out of foster care and had her first child while incarcerated. She didn't know who the father was. "I think he was Hispanic," she once told me.

Jennifer was given opportunities. We first met her when she attended The Mission Church at City of Refuge as a ten-year-old with her foster family, and she was a hot mess. She could be sappy sweet and affectionate one minute, dark and reclusive the next, then instantaneously explode into a fit of anger that would traumatize everyone in the room. Different personalities and tones of voice would emanate with no forewarning that change was on the way. We tried to meld her in with the other kids. Big mistake. She had the same chance to learn in Kids Church as all the other kids did. She was prayed for just as they were. She was placed in school with an Individualized Education Plan, and teachers who were trained and committed to addressing her emotional and mental health needs. Jennifer was the recipient of love and care, but none of it could fully repair the damage that had resulted from years of trauma and abuse.

When Jennifer aged out of the foster system, she turned to the streets and a hard life of homelessness, addiction, and selling herself to get food and support her habits. When her first child was born, a baby boy whom she named Elisha, her former foster mom took him home from the hospital, and Jennifer was sent back to jail. Because she was a single parent trying to raise several other special needs kids, the foster mom, Paula, turned to us for help. My wife and I agreed to take Elisha into our home under a legal guardianship arrangement. He lived with us for several months, until I convinced his mother to allow me to facilitate his adoption by a young couple who could not have children.

Upon her release from jail, I picked Jennifer up and took her to a Christian addiction recovery program, where she had housing, food, clothing, medical care, educational opportunities, and counseling. I committed to raise money and pay her fees for as long as she would stay. I made sure to take her to a place that was far removed from the environments and people she was familiar with. It took her two weeks to wreck the house and beat the stew out of the program director, landing her back behind bars. "That bitch thought she could tell me what to do," was her explanation. Nobody was going to tell Jennifer Johnson what to do. Another opportunity squandered.

This time she spent only a few days in jail and did not call me when she was released. A few weeks later, I heard from her when she needed money to pay her "room bill." I figured it was her pimp forcing her to come up with cash in addition to what she was already bringing in for him, but I sent it anyway. If it would prevent a beating, I would do it.

The next time I heard from Jennifer, her second child had been born. She was absolutely giddy as she described the beautiful baby girl and told me of her plans to marry the baby's father, a paying customer, and to live happily ever after in a three-bedroom ranch with a white picket fence, or something like that. She had applied for a job at a fast-food restaurant as a cook and utility person and was confident she would be hired.

Within a month, the father of her child had put Jennifer out, had taken out a restraining order against her, and had been granted full custody of the baby by the court. I went to visit him, and he explained that he lived in fear for his life and for that of his little girl as long as Jennifer was in the house. Because of her extensive criminal record and history of drug abuse and mental health episodes, the court stripped her of all parental rights. Opportunity lost.

I prayed for God to heal Jennifer, but he didn't. I don't know why, and I can't think about it for very long or I will get confused and angry. Awhile back, Bruce coined the phrase "Opportunity Injustice," and if it ever applied to anyone, it applied to Jennifer. Before the beautiful, innocent child had a chance to start her life, much less enjoy the big moments of birthday parties, Christmas mornings, graduations, engagement, and marriage, she was robbed. Her emotions were shattered beyond repair, her understanding of the beautiful human characteristic of sexuality twisted into something perverse and awful, and her ability to think rationally was stolen by selfish thieves. As a lonely child who didn't trust the adults in her support system and without an understanding of real love, she was like a solitary pine sapling trying to withstand an earthquake, avalanche, tornado, and wildfire, all at the same time. She never had a chance.

On a nondescript Thursday morning, the 20th of September, 2018, Jennifer Johnson walked out from under a bridge in Gainesville, Georgia, where she had been living for a while, and made her way to the nearby railroad track. She knew the train schedule, and at 5 a.m. she stood on the track and awaited the train she knew would soon arrive. According to witnesses, she stood calmly and faced the train, seemingly very ready to make her exit. Then she was gone.

When I started this story, I indicated that Jennifer's death was her success. That may sound like a great paradox, but I believe that sometimes the Almighty looks at a person and says, *You've had enough. I'm going to save you from what's coming.* Her exodus from this world was her rescue, and I am compelled to think that our prayers that she would be rescued, and healed, played a part.

I grew up surrounded by people who proclaimed that suicide is a guaranteed pass to eternal damnation, and maybe it is in certain situations. I don't presume to know how eternal things work, and I stopped playing God a while back. However, I have yet to encounter the individual who can convince me that a loving, kind, benevolent, merciful God, who purports to be our Father, would sentence someone whose life on earth was a living hell to separation from him in the next life, especially if the blame for their issues lies at someone else's feet. That's not justice.

Jennifer was neglected, abused, exploited, molested, and rejected. The result was a broken and confused little girl who was never able to find light at the end of her dark tunnel. I'm sad, but I'm glad she's gone, because I know her suffering is over.

Jennifer Lynn Johnson
January 10, 1986—September 20, 2018

* * *

It is important for us to highlight the stories of people who have overcome huge obstacles, broken down barriers, and built momentum toward a good and stable life, but it is also important to talk about Jennifer, Dennis, Michael, Gloria,

191

and many others who were damaged beyond repair and could never fully find stability and normalcy. Their lives were valuable and their stories meaningful, and they offer us lessons that can help us as much as the ones that leave us at their conclusions with a feeling of warmth and satisfaction. The definition of success in modern society is "the accomplishment of an aim or purpose." However, there is an archaic definition that describes success as "the good *or bad* outcome of an undertaking." The point is that a story can have a bad outcome but still stands as a success if positive lessons are learned from it.

Sometimes my theology clashes with the practical daily experience I have lived and witnessed in others. My theology says that God is a loving father who wants the best for his children at all times. My experience says that he doesn't always provide what's best, at least not what's best by my definition, even to those who cry out to him and ask for it. My theology says that God is all-powerful, knew us all before we were put together in our mothers' wombs, and is capable of repairing all our brokenness. My experience says that many people, even those who ask him to fix them, do not receive the answers or the healing they are looking for.

The strain between my theology and my experience requires that I make a decision to deny God because his ways do not align with my theology, or to trust God because I realize the problem may lie in my theology rather than in his ways. When I take a careful look at his words and his ways,

I realize that they have never included promises or guarantees that our lives would be free from pain, suffering, loss, hardship, disappointment, or death. As a matter of fact, there are many guarantees that we *will* experience these things. We live in a broken world and brokenness is the order of the day. He never promises to remove the dark valleys; he only offers to be our companion as we walk through them.

It is only by trading my theology for God's ways that I can reconcile the suffering of his children and see any value in it. Knowing his ways helps me to understand that sometimes the best answer is to remove the child from the pain rather than removing the pain from the child. Knowing his ways reminds me that he knows what's coming tomorrow, next week, next month and year, and I don't. Knowing his ways teaches me that his mercy extends beyond this natural life on planet earth and frees me from thinking inside the limited context of our entrance and exit as human beings. Knowing his ways changes my perception of success.

14

God's Not Dead . . . And Neither Is Anton

The essential thing in heaven and earth is . . .
that there should be long obedience in the same direction;
there thereby results, and has always resulted in the long run,
something which has made life worth living.
—NIETZSCHE

....

ANTON

We sat in a booth at McDonald's. He fought back emotion and said, "Jeff, you've gotta help me. If you don't help me, I'm gonna die."

"I will," I said. "You just have to do what I tell you."

"I'll do anything," he said. And he meant it.

JEFF AND TRACY

The movie was over and I was ready to go. I never stay for the credits—what's the point? But my wife is different from me and seems to genuinely enjoy many things that nearly give me a nervous breakdown—Christmas in July movies, news about the British royal family, packing thirteen outfits for a five-day trip—just to name a few. She wanted to watch the credits and enjoy the accompanying music because, well, I don't know why.

The film was called *God's Not Dead* and was of good quality and enjoyable. I agreed with its tenets and still do. We absorbed the entirety of the movie, including the credits, and were preparing to finally leave the theater, when the following message popped onto the screen: "Text 'God's Not Dead' to everyone in your contacts." *Oh, that's cute*, I thought. *What a brilliant marketing scheme to promote the movie.*

As I was processing the concept in my brain and wondering who came up with the idea, I noticed Tracy vigorously tapping away at her phone, something that is not uncommon but was somewhat interesting as we tried to navigate through a crowd and get to the car.

"You're not sending that message to all your contacts, are you?" I asked, condescendingly.

"Of course. We were instructed to, so we need to do it."

"I'm not doing that. People will think I'm nuts. Besides, most of my contacts already know God's not dead and are aware of the movie. They don't need me to tell them."

"Well, you do what you want. I'm following the instructions."

"What if the message had said, 'Jump off the nearest cliff'? Would you follow the instructions?"

She gave me her *You're an idiot* look and kept tapping.

196

AL

Why do bad things happen to good people? Why do children have to suffer because of the bad decisions, irresponsibility, or poor behavior of adults? Why are some people seemingly sentenced to misery and pain through no fault of their own? These questions are common in every culture in the world and are often used to support atheism or agnosticism. The premise is that a fair and loving God would not subject his children to the unfairness of suffering; therefore, the existence of a fair and loving God is inconceivable.

For more than thirty years, I have served as a missionary, pastor, and nonprofit administrator, and have never been able to give an adequate answer to questions about the suffering of innocent human beings. Like most leaders in such positions, I can manufacture explanations that make me sound intelligent or intuitive, but I always walk away feeling like I have only tried to make myself look smart but have not really helped the hearers. I suspect the hearers have felt the same way. Al Andrews helped me with this.

I met Al at a horse ranch in Colorado where my wife and I attended a couple's retreat. Al is a counselor in Nashville and was the guest speaker at the retreat. He and his wife, Nita, presented material that can make a bad marriage good or a good marriage better, but I immediately recognized that the principles they discussed are relevant to any person in any life situation—young or old, married or single, rich or poor, PhD or GED.

ANTON

Before Anton Childers was wiped clean by the nurse in the labor and delivery room where he was born, mountainous obstacles to a happy life loomed over his tiny frame. He was born to a woman who did not want children and who would see him as an interruption and an inconvenience to her life. Her resentment, coupled with mental health issues, would result in physical, mental, and emotional abuse that began during his infancy and grew more intense and violent as time went on. When Anton was a toddler, she parted ways with his father and demonstrated her vengeful nature by refusing to allow him to see his son for the next five years.

Born diminutive in size and with a cleft palate, severe dental problems, and structural deficiencies in his ears, Anton was targeted by bullies at a young age and had to learn to fight early on. His older brother became his caregiver and protector as they dealt with the poverty, neglect, and abuse that characterized life with their mother. They were often hungry and cold and were not allowed to have friends. She frequently terrorized them with beatings and threats, and once she shoved the barrel of a gun into Anton's mouth when he resisted his dishwashing chore.

Anton, as do all kids, had an innate desire to know his father and lived with an intuition that his father was a good person. At five years old his wish was granted, and he learned that his dad was retired from the army and was still an active reservist. He had a drinking problem but had enrolled in AA

198

and was genuinely trying to get better. He was already over fifty years of age, having fathered Anton when he was forty-six. They met and fell into a good father-son relationship that lasted for ten years. Then tragedy struck. The elder Childers suffered catastrophic heart failure and did not survive. Anton was left without his sole source of stability.

JEFFERY B.

I suppose that upon sending a group message of any sort to every number on a contact list, one should be ready for a myriad of responses. After all, some numbers may belong to persons you once loved but now despise, or vice-versa. Others may belong to total strangers because new phones have been obtained and new numbers assigned. Still others could be family members or friends who will enjoy the opportunity for a sarcastic jab.

Following Tracy's mass distribution of "God's Not Dead," she received mostly affirming responses, replies such as "Amen!" "That's right!" and "Preach!" However, at least one recipient was not happy about the news. "If you text me again, you're going to find out if he's dead or not!" the recipient shot back.

By far the most significant response to the text came on day four after the message went out. Tracy was sitting in the car line to pick up kids from school when her phone rang.

"Hello."

"Yes, someone texted me from this number and said, 'God's not dead.' Can you tell me why you did that?"

She explained about the movie and about the challenge to send the message to her entire contact list.

"Well, I think maybe God is trying to say something to me. You see, I was on a call to a suicide hotline when the message came through. I was speaking to a counselor about my depression and the serious consideration I have been giving to ending my life. My phone pinged and I looked down to see the message 'God's not dead.' I don't know what's going on here."

They had a long conversation, and she figured out that Jeffery had at some time in the past attended a Friday night support group I helped to lead at a local church. Afterwards, he had questions regarding the content from the session and asked someone for my number. They did not have it but passed along Tracy's number and told him he could reach me through her. He called us once while we were traveling, and Tracy subsequently stored his number in her phone, setting him up to be an unwitting participant in the *God's Not Dead* challenge.

AL

At the retreat in Colorado, Al Andrews presented four words that outline the life of every human being. They are as follows, with a brief explanation for each one:

Innocence—Every baby is born into Innocence. They are not guilty of anything, nor do they have the capacity to manage the contrast between good and evil.

Tragedy—At some point in life, every human being will face tragedy. The Tragedy will negatively impact the Innocence.

Contending—When tragedy comes, the person will be forced to Contend with it, one way or the other. Contending may include a wide range of emotions, reactions, and behaviors, but even to do nothing is a form of Contending.

Resolution—There will, inevitably, be a Resolution to the Tragedy, and the Resolution will be dictated by the Contending. In other words, how you Contend will determine the course of your post-Tragedy life.

ANTON

Just like every other human, Anton Childers was born into Innocence. He knew nothing of hatred, greed, lust, abuse, bitterness, fear, addiction, or deception. His heart was pure and his mind was clean, but Tragedy came early. The selfishness of adults arrived before he could feed himself or put together a sentence. As a baby, he began to witness human brokenness and to be taught by example the wrong way to Contend. There was the cursing and fighting, the abuse of alcohol and drugs, the illicit sexual behavior. Brokenness and dysfunction were passed along to the next generation like emotional cyanide. By the time he entered eighth grade, he carried an explosive temper, was living in perpetual homelessness, and was perfectly positioned to carry the legacy of addiction into the next generation. After all, this is how he was taught to Contend.

Anton was in Atlanta the day he got the news that his father had suddenly passed away. By the time he reached his father's home a hundred miles away, the vultures had swept in and nearly everything Mr. Childers owned was gone. The things Anton would have cherished—guns, tools, military gear, and the like—had been swept up by greedy relatives and friends and were likely on their way to flea markets and pawn shops. One rifle and one shotgun were left, but an impoverished boy could only hold on to them for a short while. They eventually made their way to a pawn shop shelf as well, and disappeared forever.

JEFFERY B.

"I think the kids should audition for a play," Tracy randomly declared one day.

"Excuse me?"

"Yeah, the arts council is doing a rock-n-roll version of *Romeo and Juliet*, and I think we should let them try out. I think they would enjoy it."

I know my wife and had no doubt that there was much more to this appeal than she was presenting in her initial sales pitch. We had very busy lives and the play would involve several weeks of long rehearsals. We didn't need anything else to do. I knew that she had continued to communicate with Jeffery, serving as a lay counselor of sorts, listening to his woes and praying with him. Had I not been well aware that Jeffery was not at all interested in women, I may have been jealous.

As well, I had learned that Jeffery was attempting to launch a theater company in our area and was the director of the aforementioned play.

Upon full disclosure, I was made aware that Jeffery was recruiting actors, singers, and dancers for the play, and Tracy saw it as an opportunity to support his efforts in an attempt to grow a trusting relationship between him and our family. She saw it as a chance to reinforce her "God's Not Dead" claim by extending kindness and benevolence in his direction, which required the investment of time and attention. Was I to say no to that?

ANTON

By age seventeen Anton had been kicked out of school, was known to every law enforcement officer in the county, and had fathered his first child. He was drinking daily and had been rejected by the mother of his child and her family. The vicious cycles of poverty, addiction, and broken family relationships he had grown up in manifested themselves in his life in dramatic and destructive fashion. As a teen boy, the collateral damage from his lifestyle and behavior had already grown to a landfill of brokenness, and the worst was yet to come.

Anton's couch-to-couch existence finally landed him at the home of Sheila Green, a foster parent of sorts, who opened her home to wayward and wandering young people, but who expected them to work and help pay the bills. Her newest resident was glad to have shelter and had never been avoidant to work. He got a job as an ironworker and began to bring good money into the house; however, the Green family struggled with its own varieties of dysfunction and addiction, and Anton became even more embedded in his problems. By age nineteen, he was in the category of "functioning alcoholic," and had fathered his second child. The mother of the child was Sheila's own daughter, Karen, and the baby was a boy they named Deven.

DEVEN

Tracy began taking three of our children to rehearsals for *Rock-n-Roll Romeo and Juliet.* A raucous atmosphere inundated the room as kids and teenagers ignored directions, while a live band thumped out songs by Dire Straits, Lou Reed, and Elvis Presley. Jeffery moved about the stage and barked out commands, but few in the cast were listening. It was obvious that his blood pressure was rising, as his voice became shrill and the skin on his neck evolved from pink to crimson. Finally, his patience ran out and he bellowed, "Shut up and get to your places! We can't get anything done like this!"

Silence fell over the room, and the wide-eyed team of youngsters began to nervously shuffle to their spots. Suddenly, a well-built and strikingly handsome young man in a white T-shirt stepped from the shadows at the back of the stage, both fists issuing from the front of his body and both middle fingers standing at attention. He silently mouthed the meaning behind the two-finger salute, but Jeffery was paying him no mind. The young man strutted to his spot on the stage, a cocky smile lingering on his lips.

May I introduce Deven Green, Anton's second child and first son.

Tracy was struck by the brazenness and profaneness of the boy, but was also drawn to him, perhaps because he reminded her of herself when she was his age. She grew up in a broken home with an alcoholic father and could identify with the anger and resentment she witnessed from Deven. She saw resistance to authority that seemed familiar, and though she now had many years under her belt as a respectful Christian lady, she couldn't help but feel a connection to someone who was living where she once lived.

The dust finally settled, and it became apparent that Deven was the main character, Romeo, himself. When the rehearsal was over, Tracy made her way to where he was and introduced herself. Beginning that night, she became a mother figure to Deven Green and made it her mission to make him feel accepted and valued. She invited him to our Friday night group, and he showed up. When it was time for me to speak, I passed out party hats and noisemakers and told them that everyone was welcome at the party. I told them that Jesus liked to party with people who had addictions, bad attitudes, and anger issues, because he knew he could help them. I told them I want to be like Jesus, so no one is excluded from my party. I told them if they would jump in and party with us that the addictions, bad attitudes, and anger issues would start to fall off, and they would find tremendous freedom and peace that they never knew existed. I told them we loved them.

For many weeks, Deven showed up at The Mission on Friday nights, and most of the time he brought friends. Our kids performed in the play with him, but when the play was over, he kept coming. Deven became part of the family, participating not only in the Friday night group sessions, but hanging out with us at social and community outreach events, and even coming to our house, sometimes unannounced.

Some months after we first met, on a Friday night at The Mission, Deven nervously approached me and asked to talk. He said that he would like to invite his father to a group session, but that he needed to warn me that his dad was a severe alcoholic and would likely be drunk when he came. He said he understood if I would rather him not come, if I, you know, was afraid there might be a disturbance or something.

"What's your dad's name?" I asked.

"His name is Anton. Anton Childers."

"You tell Anton Childers," I said with a smile, "that everyone is invited to the party."

AL

As Al elaborated on the four words, especially on the significance of how we Contend after Tragedy, I couldn't help but reflect on all the people I have known who Contended wrongly and whose lives were negatively impacted, or totally destroyed, as a result. I thought of Harold, who nurtured the bitterness that grew in him as a result of abuse by his father, allowed it to grow into seething hatred, and murdered a man over a place in line for pancakes and sausage. He is spending the rest of his life in prison.

I thought of Gloria, who Contended with cheap wine and crack cocaine, trying to numb the pain that resulted from losing a child. On a freezing night in Atlanta, she sat in an armchair in an unheated, abandoned house, and froze to death. They found her sitting upright and staring forward, a tear frozen on her cheek. She had a thin and dirty blanket across her legs, under which her fingers still gripped a glass bottle.

I thought of Tandy, whose grandfather began to sexually abuse her when she was twelve, but who had the chance to Contend well when she was mandated by the court to the House of Cherith program for survivors of sex trafficking and exploitation. She was loved and cared for, but she chose to Contend by leaving the program in the middle of the night and returning to the people who had controlled her for the previous few years. As far as I know, she is still alive, but is living in a dark and evil world of abuse and horror. Perhaps she will one day come home and allow us to Contend on her behalf again.

Anton Childers was drunk, as predicted, when he walked through the door of The Mission the Friday night following my conversation with Deven. He wore a gray pinstripe suit because he thought he was "going to church." He was not loud or belligerent, but he seemed to attempt to hide his intoxication with deliberate speech and cautious movements.

"Help yourself to some food," I said. He grabbed a plate and made his way along the bar we had set up with snack mix and cake, but when he got to the end of the bar, the plate was still empty.

"Are you not hungry?" I asked. "You didn't get any food."

"I'm hungry," he replied, "but y'all ain't got no food. This ain't real food."

"I'll tell you what," I said as I patted him on the shoulder, "if you come back next week, I'll have a spread of 'real food' out here just for you."

"We'll see," he said, and took a seat. Let the Contending begin.

Jeffery B

Bruce sometimes says, "Some come to see. Some come for a season. Some come to stay." Jeffery continued to direct plays in our town, and my kids continued to participate. Eventually, Jeffery started attending our Friday night group sessions as well, but his involvement was limited.

It seemed he wanted to dabble his feet in the water but did not want to take the deep dive. He had received his party invitation but would only sit on the perimeter and observe instead of putting on his party hat and joining the celebration in earnest. He wanted to Contend, but to do so in varying ways—sometimes absorbing the Truth, meditating on the Scriptures, and worshiping his Creator. Other times he Contended by relying on philosophies, ideas, opinions and theories, and flaunting his immoral behavior. During these times, he became argumentative and haughty. The results were deeper levels of depression and confusion.

Eventually, he stopped coming and faded out of our lives.

ANTON

Since he first started to sip alcohol in his early teens, Anton would count intoxicating drink as his first love. When he married Karen at age nineteen, he broke up with drinking, and when Katen was born, his resolution to live alcohol-free strengthened. He was married and was raising two of his children, working steadily and making decent money, and taking the family to church on Sundays. Life was good, and then Tragedy struck again. The brokenness from both their lives started to manifest itself, becoming a tale of the blind leading the blind, and their world fell apart. He returned to his first love, the bottle, and the next twenty years would be dominated by his involvement with it. Not long after he realized the marriage to Karen was unraveling, they found out she was pregnant again. She gave birth to Anton's fourth child, a daughter they named Bridget. The marriage ended in destructive fashion, and Karen took custody of the kids. She refused to allow the father of her children to see them, and his emotions spiraled even further out of control. Karen's mother,

Sheila, eventually adopted them, but always at the root of the relationships was manipulation and scheming. More Tragedy.

The relationship with Karen had offered Anton hope that his life may not be destined for failure after all. He was married to a beautiful woman. He was committed to being a good father. He was growing in his faith and becoming more stable as a man. He seemed to be breaking destructive cycles, but Tragedy has a way of derailing good intentions, especially if instability still lingers like a fault line. When things shift violently, the unstable person may not Contend so well.

The next twenty years were like a war movie, with explosion-filled battles and lulls that were always seasoned with profaneness, addiction, and debauchery. Another failed marriage and an aggravated assault conviction. Another son born into the turmoil of family brokenness. Mountains of unpaid child support accumulating between two wives and four children. Multiple run-ins with the law that resulted in jail time and probation. Anton once jokingly said that they could re-surface all the roads in the county with the money he had paid in fines and probation fees. It's barely a joke.

Anton was forty years old when he first walked into The Mission on that Friday night. He reeked of alcohol and walked a little unstably. His life consisted of rising early each day and having a forty-ounce malt liquor for breakfast. He worked at a pallet factory and was allowed to live in a squalid little house that was owned by his boss. Each workday he would have two more forties while on his lunch break. That's right, by early afternoon, Anton would have consumed 120 ounces of the cheapest rot-gut booze that money can buy. Clocking out at five p.m. meant clocking in to the most serious drinking of all. Every night he drank until he passed out. The next morning, it started again.

When Deven proposed the idea of inviting his father to The Mission, he made it known that he loved his dad, and that his dad was a good person, but a good person with problems. The perspective of others in the group was different. *Deven's a good kid but his dad is the town drunk* was the general consensus. One person offered that the common expectation around town was that Anton would one day be found dead on the sidewalk, and it would surprise no one. He was known, or known about, by nearly everyone in town, and the opinions were not good.

We continued to prepare full meals on Fridays, just so Anton could enjoy some "real food." I started to see his benevolent heart as he jumped in to help clean up, set up chairs, or take out the garbage. One week I announced that we would have Italian food that coming Friday, and that I would bring the main dishes. I asked the attendees to bring items to go with spaghetti and lasagna, such as salad, bread, and desserts. Anton showed up with fish sticks. At least he brought something. At least he was consuming something besides malt liquor. When I asked him how fish sticks align with Italian food, he said he was aware that Italian food comes from Italy and that Italy is situated on the Mediterranean Sea; therefore, seafood should go well with Italian food. I told him I wasn't aware that fish sticks actually qualify as seafood, but okay. He popped them into the microwave and had mushy microwave fish sticks with his spaghetti. Priceless.

A few weeks passed and I was giving serious thought to the next step for Anton. I decided to offer him the chance to go on a three-day retreat in the North Georgia mountains. He hesitantly agreed, knowing that he would not have access to booze or cigarettes while he was there. At his level of dependence on alcohol, it is deemed medically inadvisable for a person to go that long without consuming it or taking a counteractive drug. There was a chance that Anton would get to the retreat and have an episode—anything from violent vomiting, fever, chills, hallucinations, extreme anxiety, or seizures, which could be life-threatening. If a long-term, severe alcoholic decides to go cold-turkey, they should do so under medical supervision.

Anton decided to go, and although it was tough, I believe it was a monumental step toward his healing. Not long after the retreat, he called and asked if he could meet with me to discuss some very important matters.

We sat in a booth at McDonald's. He fought back emotion and said, "Jeff, you've gotta help me. If you don't help me, I'm gonna die."

"I will," I said. "You just have to do what I tell you."

"I'll do anything," he said. And he meant it.

After a few days of discussing the logistics and

practicalities of Anton's consent to enter a long-term residential treatment program, I loaded him up and headed to a place called Mighty Man in South Georgia. We had his wife, Sherrie, comfortably situated in an efficiency apartment and had given her a car. We reassured them both that she would be taken care of and the bills would be paid. We cleaned out their old house and notified his boss that he needed about a year of time off.

When we got to the entrance to the Mighty Man property outside Davisboro, I stopped the car and told Anton to get out.

"What for?" he asked.

"This is where you smoke your last cigarette," I replied.

"Oh, they don't allow smoking here?"

"No, freedom from addiction means freedom from all of it. Now, light up and enjoy."

He took out a cigarette and put fire to it. He took three or four drags, threw it on the ground, and stomped it out. He handed me the rest of the pack and said, "Let's go." It was the last cigarette he would light, and after twenty-five years of living with a cigarette between his lips or fingers, he never wanted one again.

At Mighty Man, the withdrawals slammed into Anton like a locomotive. He spent more than two weeks dealing with sickness like he'd never experienced. Massive headaches and convulsions wracked his body as he spent long hours writhing on his bed. It was as if the alcohol was a living entity that had its claws around his vital organs, refusing to let go without the fiercest of fights. He burned with fever, shook with chills, and drenched his sheets with sweat. At times he asked God to take him, and at times he was convinced God was honoring the request. Staff persons offered to take him to the hospital, but he was committed to waging war until he broke free or died. He broke free!

Anton spent the next ten months breaking free. He plowed through the steps in his process of healing—classes, group therapy, and individual counseling, Bible studies and worship, service and outreach, and work on the Mighty Man farm—and graduated three months ahead of schedule. He came home a new man.

SHERRIE

When Anton arrived home from Mighty Man, Sherrie was waiting. As a matter of fact, she had been waiting since the day she married him—waiting for him to be the leader their family needed, waiting for a husband who valued her more than the bottle, waiting for order to rise from the chaos. To say the least, their relationship had been initiated for the wrong reasons, but she loved him and wanted the marriage to work.

Her ex-husband was now involved with Anton's ex-wife. She had two children and Anton had a son, but the relationships with their former partners were characterized by hostility and the kids were being kept from them. Both Sherrie and Anton were left with no one, so they turned to each other, somewhat out of attraction, and a whole lot out of retaliation. They were building on a faulty foundation, but at least they had someone to accompany them through the misery that was their lives.

The only Anton Sherrie had ever known was one of drunken foolishness and problems. She was accustomed to the stench of cheap booze and stale tobacco on his breath, and to the explosions of anger and severe mood swings. As the day approached for him to return home, she dealt with a mixture of hopefulness and anxiety. She had visited him at Mighty Man and had attended his graduation, but was true transformation really possible? He would come home to a borrowed apartment, unemployment, the same influences and temptations he had left nearly a year before, and a deep sense of disappointment and dissatisfaction with his family relationships. It is common for stresses such as these to serve as triggers to relapse. She wondered which trigger might set him off.

Sherrie knew what she wanted and knew the direction she wanted her marriage to go, but she was uncertain how to get there. Things had always been volatile, unpredictable, and unstable. She was now dealing with the idea that her husband was in the best condition he'd been in since they met, but with an underlying sense of uncertainty laced with a tinge of dread.

Then he was home.

ANTON AND MIRACLES

It has been five years since Anton Childers dropped the

unsmoked cigarette at the Mighty Man gate and said, "Let's go." He completed the program as a star participant and was invited to stay on in a leadership position, but he had a wife at home and many fences to mend with family and acquaintances. He was ready to face everyone and everything that had ever hurt him or that he had hurt. There would be no ducking and dodging, only real life that would begin amidst a pile of rubble. His response was, "Let's go."

When his former boss and landlord found out Anton was back in town, he immediately sued him for back rent totaling thousands of dollars. An already disastrous credit profile was now pummeled by a judgment against him, and he would be facing garnishment of wages as soon as employment was secured. Finding a job in a town where his reputation didn't precede him would prove to be a challenge. He owed tens of thousands of dollars in back child support to the two ex-wives, both of whom hated his guts. He was still well known to local police, and not for good reasons; therefore, he had to mark his steps more carefully than more benign citizens for fear that wrong assumptions would be made. Relationships with the three kids he had with Karen were shaky, and he didn't even know where his youngest child was. Hairline triggers quivered under the pressure of his circumstances, but Anton stood firm.

Without faith in a higher power, there is no way to adequately explain what has happened in the life of Anton Childers over the past five years. It can only be categorized as miraculous. He obtained employment, first as a janitor at a nursing home, then as a lift operator at a sawmill and lumber yard, then as the Maintenance Director at City of Refuge. With each change his responsibilities grew, his skill set was utilized in a more productive fashion, and his pay increased. However, the most important work Anton has done, and continues to do, is to help other addicts and alcoholics get into recovery programs and find their own pathways to transformation. He is pursuing certification as an addiction counselor in the state of Georgia and will continue to use his own miraculous story of healing and recovery to motivate others, but now as a certified professional.

After a few payments, the judgment against him by his former boss was dismissed by the court. When Anton needed a passport to go on an overseas mission trip but could not get approval because of the unpaid child support, both ex-wives voluntarily walked into the local office and completed paperwork to relieve him of any obligation to pay it. Because of the time she had lost with her two sons, Sherrie was granted custody of them by her ex-husband, and it happened without a fight. Anton's ex-wife took the lead in reconciling the relationship and making sure he had a chance to build a relationship with their son. In Anton's words, "You can't make this stuff up."

In the spring of 2022, Anton received a call from a woman who identified herself as the niece of his father. She told him she was coming to town and wondered if they might meet for a meal and conversation. He hesitantly agreed, not knowing what the motivation was. He met her at Chili's on a Sunday afternoon where they dined and had cordial conversation. As mentioned previously, when Anton was born, his father was forty-six years old, making many of his cousins much older than him. Such was the case with the relative with whom he was now visiting. He enjoyed the time and sharing his short list of good memories, but mostly listened to her stories about his dad.

When the meal was over, his cousin walked with him to the parking lot and asked him to come to her car. She opened the trunk and took out a container. She raised the lid to reveal a beautiful nickel-plated 22 caliber revolver in a lovely leather holster. "I want you to have this," she said. "It belonged to your father. When I was a little girl, maybe seven or eight, he told me he wanted me to have it. I never understood why he gave it to me at that age, and me being a girl, but I think it should be yours." She held it out to him, and with trembling hands, he took it and began to weep.

I suppose Anton's cousin left Chili's assuming he became emotional because he had received a gift that had belonged to his father. That was certainly part of it, but only a very small part. Anton's mind was swirling with a story that began before he was born. His perspective is that years before he was conceived, God orchestrated a plan for him to receive confirmation of his love and providence in a Chili's parking lot on a Sunday afternoon in the spring of 2022. And it happened during his forty-sixth year. When his dad was forty-six, he gave life to a son, but the son was cheated out of life with his father. When his father died, the only thing Anton wanted was something significant that he could treasure and remember him by. The cousin may not have understood, but Anton understood very well. It was an exclamation point on the transformational work that had been in process for the past six years.

Anton is enjoying life with Sherrie, Deven, Katen, Bridget, Christian, and the newest addition—grandson Andrew. A cataclysmic shift in his method of Contending has resulted in new and abundant life. His declaration to me, "If you don't help me, I'm gonna die," was a statement of surrender, and when he surrendered, God took over. In the spring of 2021, it was discovered that he had a leaking heart valve that would require open heart surgery. I can't help but think about the possibility, or probability, or certainty, that he would not be alive today had he not changed his method of Contending. The predictions would have become reality— he would have been found dead on the sidewalk or somewhere, and no one would have been surprised. Instead, an alcohol-free, tobacco-free, anger-free, bitterness-free, unfor-giveness-free Anton Childers addressed the problem with a cleansed body and a clear head. He listened to the doctors, had the surgery, and is here for his grandson.

God's not dead, and neither is Anton, and I agree, "You can't make this stuff up."

15

Follow the Shoes, Connect the Dots

*The mystery of human existence lies
not in just staying alive, but in finding
something to live for.*
—FYODOR DOSTOYEVSKY

....

Note: To protect the identities of donors who wish to remain anonymous, the names of the persons in this story have been changed.

WHY WAS THIS MAN, this preacher, asking for Jeremy's shoes? Why not ask for cash contributions to purchase shoes for the poor? Why not implore the listeners to come back the next day with shoes they had dug out of their closets or scrounged from dirty shoe bins in their garages? Why the shoes he and fifteen hundred other attendees at the young adult conference had on at the moment? Why now? Why here? Why shoes? Why, why, why? Jeremy didn't want to give away his shoes. They were his favorites. They were comfortable and had been acquired at premium cost. He sat on the padded chair in the modern and beautiful worship center and wrestled with the idea. Recently, I heard someone say that you can never connect the dots by looking forward; rather, you can only see how the dots were connected by looking backward. I was intrigued by this declaration, so much so that I went to the web and printed a connect-the-dots sheet from an educational website. I wanted to test the theory to see if it was in fact true. I placed the sheet on the desk in front of me and began to scrutinize it. No matter how hard I focused, or from which angle I looked, or how long I stared, I could make out nothing but dots and numbers on a white piece of paper. I discovered no art, no color, no beauty, only dots and numbers that would have to be negotiated one at a time for the picture to become clear.

I picked up a marker and drew a line from dot 1 to dot 2. I had to start somewhere, and to start at the beginning seemed the best idea.

To align with its twenty-fifth anniversary, City of Refuge recently launched a twenty-five-million-dollar capital campaign. Included in the monies raised so far is a million dollars from the Harris Family Foundation, but this is not their first gift to the organization. As a matter of fact, the Harris family has been supporting good works at COR for more than a dozen years and their combined gifts total over four million dollars, not to mention truckloads of high-quality household goods, clothing, and toys. Their first financial gift was the largest we had received to date and put us on the radar to be considered by other foundations and private donors. Following the initial gift, Ron and Betsy Harris decided to make generous annual contributions to support operations. Through the years they have never wavered in their commitment. The donations have always been generous and on time. In the nonprofit world, faithful and predictable support is huge.

The Harris family has been blessed with substantial resources and benevolent hearts. They support many good works around the world, and City of Refuge is blessed to be on the list of organizations they believe in. They first heard about COR from Craig, the chairman of their family foundation. Craig and his wife, Jen, had made the discovery through their kids' youth pastor and had become regular contributors and volunteers. The youth pastor was a guy named Jeremy, the guy at war with himself and a conference speaker over a pair of shoes.

It all started as Jeremy listened to the preacher as he compelled fifteen hundred young adults to bring their shoes to the middle of the room and place them on a pile. The man emphasized that true giving requires sacrifice and requires that we lay aside our comforts if we want to make others more comfortable. He knew the majority of the people in the room would be dressed decently and that shoes are paramount in the fashion portfolios of most young adults. He knew that to walk from the room, socialize in the hallways and lobbies, and exit the building to walk shoeless across the parking lot would require a mass exodus from the comfort zones most of the attendees were living in, not to mention the financial impact on young adult pocketbooks. He also knew the power of peer pressure and that some would respond out of compassion for the poor, a few would participate because they wore shoes they wouldn't mind getting rid of, but many would throw their shoes on the pile because of the response of the people around them and their desire to not be seen as selfish or uncaring. It was a brilliant strategy.

Jeremy held back to see what the response of the crowd would be. To be honest, he didn't want to give away his shoes, but he wasn't going to be "that guy" either. The response was overwhelming as young men and women made their way to the center of the room, dropped their shoes on the pile, and walked out in their socks or with bare feet.

Looking back on an exquisitely completed connect-the dots work of art, I see Jeremy's decision to remove his favorite shoes and throw them on a pile in the center of the floor as a move from dot 1 to dot 2. Little did he know that a journey had begun that would result in one homeless man receiving the blessing of a pair of donated shoes, but would also ripple out to affect thousands of people and that the value of his contribution would grow to millions of dollars.

Jeremy is the curious sort and was not satisfied to simply send off his shoes to an unknown destination and to be uninformed or underinformed of the reason for the appeal. He wanted to know where and to whom the shoes were going and what the purpose behind all of this amounted to. He went on a mission to find the person responsible for the shoe collection and subsequent distribution. A little digging produced the person's name and some effort resulted in an audience where the question was asked, "What's gonna happen with the shoes?"

"They're going to an organization on Atlanta's west side called City of Refuge" was the response. Jeremy went to work to find out more about this "City of Refuge" and how they planned to use his shoes. He found out that the organization provided transitional housing to previously homeless women and children, but that they also collected and distributed food, clothing, shoes, and household goods to homeless people and struggling families in the community. He told his wife, Megan, about it and they decided to make a trip downtown to get a first-hand look at the City of Refuge campus and to see how they might get involved. They had been struggling with the disappointment of not being able to have a child and saw this as an opportunity to perhaps fill some of the void by serving others and doing good works.

Jeremy never knew exactly who received the shoes he donated, but it really doesn't matter. He knew that his act of benevolent obedience had resulted in a spike in the quality of life for someone, and that he and Megan had discovered fulfilling work that was blessing others and enriching their own lives. He offered his aptitude and bandwidth for technology to assist City of Refuge in markedly expanding its footprint through website development and social media presence. Through the years there have been a handful of benchmark situations that have propelled the organization to the next level. Jeremy's contributions, first as a volunteer, and eventually as an employee, are among them.

More dots connected.

Sadly, many nonprofit organizations that work with homeless people or people in crisis are governed by a poverty mentality, which is to say that the lifestyle and work should be characterized by sacrifice. In other words, employees should sacrifice a decent salary because they work with the poor. Facilities should not be overly nice or well-appointed, but should manifest the drab world in which they exist and the struggling lives they serve. City of Refuge is proud to be one of the agencies in Atlanta that has flipped the script on this mentality. The core values on which the organization is built—Passion, Excellence, Dignity, and Integrity—have mandated that we operate at the highest possible level. The premise lies in believing that we are doing God's work, and if any work is worthy of our best, it is God's work.

It starts with a Passion for what we do. Passion is defined as "a strong and barely controllable emotion" (Oxford Languages). In other words, it is an internal emotional force that drives a person toward an action or mission. If Passion for a cause exists in the heart of a person or group, action is sure to follow.

At City of Refuge, the immediate and automatic

companion to Passion is Excellence. From the first encounter with the security officer at the front gate to the raised bed gardens at the very back of the property, it is our desire that there be a noticeable, exceptional quality both aesthetically and operationally. The commons areas and dining hall are clean, inviting, and beautifully decorated, with a familial rather than an institutional ambiance. The residential spaces are designed to make people feel at home rather than in a "shelter." The vocational training center compares with the best of corporate and professional environments and operates on cutting edge technology.

A strong commitment to Dignity is the motivator toward Passion and Excellence. Seeing every individual who comes on campus as just as important as the wealthiest donor pushes us to treat them with respect and to operate in a way that highlights their worth. Dignity is the reason our housing program is set up to give each single lady or mom with kids their own private room. A bunkhouse environment may provide the opportunity to serve greater numbers (it's the way we started out), but Dignity is minimized or lost when there is no privacy. Imagine a mother with three children, or a young lady re-entering society after a period of incarceration, or a scared and traumatized girl who has been rescued from sex trafficking, being escorted into her own room, a room that is freshly painted and decorated in yellow and blue, with pillows and artwork and lamps, a room that is clean and fresh and warm, a room that declares, *You're important!* Through the years, the reactions have included screams of joy, speechlessness, tears, and declarations of shock and surprise. My favorite is to hear them simply say, "This is *my* room."

At the heart of the matter is the issue of Integrity. The key to maintaining a high level of Integrity is to stay true to the mission. It goes back to our belief that we are doing God's work rather than implementing a plan that came from a business strategy or brainstorming session. We are simply stewarding a calling and the resources that come our way. We must remain obedient to the process that is set before us day by day and trust God for the results. In other words, we are not responsible for results; rather, we are only responsible to obey, and in doing so we find that the results are always more and better than we could have produced through strategy alone.

Simon Sinek has been a friend to City of Refuge for many years, and his book *Start with Why* illustrates the importance of understanding what lies behind our approach to life and work. "People don't buy *what* you do, they buy *why* you do it. And what you do simply proves what you believe," Sinek says.[1] A good understanding of why we do what we do mandates a commitment to Passion, Excellence, Dignity, and Integrity, and the daily work proves what we believe.

After giving away one pair of shoes, making an inquiry and a visit, and beginning to volunteer on a regular basis,

---

1 Simon Sinek, *Start with Why: How Great Leaders Inspire Everyone to Take Action* (New York: Portfolio, 2009).

Jeremy's next move was to share his discovery with others who could potentially make a difference.

He had been serving in ministry to the youth of his church and thought about the parents of two kids in the group. Their father, Craig, was the chairman of a family foundation that was known for supporting benevolent work around the world. Jeremy was smart and talented, but he was not wealthy. Craig, on the other hand, represented a family that was very wealthy and who had the ability to invest in the work of City of Refuge at a high level. Jeremy invited Craig and Jen for a tour and conversation on campus, and they agreed. Another dot connected.

At the next foundation meeting, Craig found it easy to present City of Refuge as a potential recipient of support. He and Jen had already given of their time, talent, and treasure and could speak firsthand to the Passion, Excellence, Dignity, and Integrity they had witnessed. It was an easy sell and the Harrises immediately agreed to make a visit downtown. A single pair of shoes led them there, shoes that had walked from dot to dot since Jeremy threw them on a pile in response to a preacher's ridiculous appeal, shoes that are still walking today.

The Harris Family Foundation made an initial gift of $750,000 and has included City of Refuge in its annual giving every year since that time, including the recent million-dollar pledge to the capital campaign.

As I sat at my desk and drew lines in sequence on my connect-the-dots worksheet, I began to see formation of a snowflake, one of the most complex and unique natural elements in all of creation. Upon completion, the dots and numbers made sense, but I could only understand it by looking backwards. In other words, obedience to the process is my assignment; someone else is responsible for the results, someone who designed the worksheet and provided a marker and requires that I simply connect one dot at a time.

Cool side note: As I mentioned previously, before coming to City of Refuge, Jeremy and Megan had been living with the disappointment of not being able to have children. They were on campus one day when a homeless man approached Megan as she stood by the water fountain in the dining hall. Perhaps he was there for a meal or a haircut or to get his blood pressure checked, or maybe to receive a pair of donated shoes. Out of the blue, he said to Megan, "Don't worry about that baby. You're going to have one. As a matter of fact, you'll have four boys, so don't worry."

The homeless prophet was not entirely accurate, but Jeremy and Megan don't mind. When I first contacted Jeremy to talk about this story, they were at Disney World with their three sons and one daughter. The art, color, and beauty of their unique snowflake continues to unfold, and it began with one decision to do something selfless, something good, a simple move to connect the first two dots.

16
The Bones
Are Good

GOD, the Master, told the dry bones,
"Watch this: I'm bringing the breath of life to you
and you'll come to life. I'll attach sinews to you,
put meat on your bones, cover you with skin, and breathe life
into you. You'll come alive and you'll realize that I am GOD!"
—EZEKIEL 37:5–6 MSG

....

"LET'S BUY IT," Bruce said, smiling. "We can do something here."

Yep, I thought, *we can get robbed. We can get shot and killed. We can get propositioned by drug dealers and prostitutes. We can get mauled by giant rats. This will be fun!*

The building was partly covered with graffiti, was infected with harmful materials such as asbestos and mold, was surrounded by weeds and debris, and was seemingly void of any heritage or potential. It was a dumping ground for people in the community who found it inconvenient to locate a garbage can. Because it stood three stories high in a neighborhood of mostly one-story homes and businesses, and a few two-story apartment buildings, it reigned as king among all the eyesores one could see from the City of Refuge gate. The address is 345 Chappell Road, just west of campus across the railroad tracks.

As I stood there nervously waiting for Bruce to say we could go, I thought about 2003 when he sent a real-estate agent to The Bluff to find a suitable property for us to acquire after we had outgrown the church building on 14th Street. For some time, we had known that the people we were serving on a daily basis were coming from Atlanta's west side, migrating down MLK, Simpson, and Bankhead, crossing Northside Drive, to seek assistance from churches and other agencies or to panhandle in more lucrative environments. Bruce decided he wanted to go to them rather than continuing to require them to come to us. Our agent, Rick Ross, found our current facility, but it wasn't the beautiful and fully functional place that it is today. Rather, the once thriving warehousing center was an empty, dirty, and toxic skeleton of what it had been in its glory days. It, too, was occupied by rats and homeless dudes, and the latter had been burning creosote-laden timbers they dragged down from the railroad track to stay warm. The whole place was a poisonous and stinky hellhole that was covered in an icky grime composed of soot and rat urine.

But, the bones were good.

In the fields of engineering, construction, and real estate, it's a phrase used when a structure seems to be in irreparable condition, but after inspection, the experts recognize that the foundation and load-bearing and exterior walls are still strong and should be retained and not demolished. In doing so, historical significance can be preserved, not to mention the money that is saved on the new construction by not having to start from the ground up.

In 2003, the property at 1300 Simpson Road was donated to City of Refuge. It had been on the market for $1.6 million, but the owner believed in our vision and generously gave it to us. It included eight acres of land with 210,000 square feet of warehouse space under one roof. It had once been a distribution center for Don Swann Industries but had been closed for more than a decade. The property was surrounded by an eight-foot fence with razor wire across the top of it. It looked like a prison. The roof leaked in a thousand places, the electrical and plumbing systems were ancient, and the small office section was covered in cobwebs and dirt. But the bones were good.

In 2017, City of Refuge purchased the three-story building at 345 Chappell Road. The Danzig was built by O. T. Bell in 1959 and was one of only three African American-owned motels in Atlanta in the 1960s. It served the clean and quiet community with lodging and amenities for forty years and was finally sold to Antioch Baptist Church in 1997. By that time the neighborhood had declined and had become dominated by drug dealers and other criminal elements. Antioch launched a program for HIV positive residents and named it Matthew's Place, but the program failed to gain traction and was soon discontinued. Nevertheless, its function to house a program for people in crisis foreshadowed what was to come. The building fell into disrepair and was abandoned to become part of the blight of the 30314 zip code, but the bones were good.

We bought the old Danzig at 345 Chappell Road, not knowing what we would do with it. Maybe it would be an investment property that we would hold until the market was stronger, then sell. Maybe we would raze the building and create a small park or playground. Maybe we would build a youth recreation center or a S.T.E.A.M. educational facility. It was our dynamic vocational training operation that finally gifted us the idea for its best and highest use.

Since moving from the church building on 14th Street to the warehouses on Simpson (which became Joseph E. Boone Blvd.), City of Refuge had provided housing, programs and services almost exclusively to women and children. We were not opposed to helping men, and we did so with food, clothing, medical services, hygiene products, and placement into addiction recovery programs. But women and kids were our target when it came to housing and wraparound services. They seemed more vulnerable, and we focused on them unapologetically.

Then came the Workforce Innovation Hub. In 2019, we built a state-of-the-art vocational training center and began to offer a variety of training options and to place graduates into Atlanta's workforce by hosting job fairs and collaborating with employment partners. Our culinary arts program had been in existence for a dozen years, and the same year we bought The

Danzig we had launched an auto technician training program in cooperation with NAPA Auto Parts. The Hub greatly expanded our capacity for training and the number of students we could accommodate, and the scholarships were open to women *and* men. Offering job training to women who were benefiting from free housing and food, free daycare and after-school programming for their children, and many other services, made perfect sense and was an immediate success. Making the program work for men proved to be more challenging. With no housing benefit, many were trying to figure out how to work enough hours to be able to pay rent and eat while being involved in a full-time training program. We wanted to provide educational opportunities to guys who were returning to society from incarceration, but they needed somewhere to live. A few of the men who applied for the program were actually homeless. Others lived some distance from our campus and faced the challenge of making an 8 a.m. class by walking or depending on public transportation, not to mention the burden of paying $90 per month for a MARTA card.

As with so many things through the years, the answer came not in brainstorming sessions or think tank meetings or vision-casting seminars; rather, the need became the call, and the answer opened up like a parting of the clouds. We had begun to serve men in a powerfully important way, but the efforts were being hindered by a housing crisis for many of them. We owned an old motel just around the corner. We would turn the motel into housing for men. We would take the strong bones of the Danzig and build something transformational.

Soon after this decision was made, our Executive Team gathered inside the building at 345 Chappell to talk and pray. We avoided holes in the floors and timbers that were leaning precariously and found a spot that seemed relatively safe. I looked around the circle at the fantastic group of friends and co-laborers and knew that we had the right team at the right time for the right purpose: Bruce, our founder and CEO; Bill, VP of Finance and Human Resources; Scott, VP of Development and Strategy; Darrell, VP of Community Revitalization. These are men with invaluable talent, experience, and a huge bandwidth for what they do, but most of all, they are men who are committed to the COR core values of Passion, Excellence, Dignity, and Integrity.

Also in that circle was Greg Washington, VP of Re-entry, and the man who will serve as Director of The 345 Housing Program for Men. He is most certainly the right person for the job because of his professionalism, experience, and spirit of compassion and service, but mostly because he will be able to identify with the men who will live there.

In April 2006, Greg walked through the City of Refuge gate for the first time. He carried with him a history of destruction and a cache of reasons why he should never be able to do well in life. He had just been released from prison after serving a long sentence for drug trafficking.

He had no money, no car, no home, and only a high

school education. His acquaintances in the city were thugs and criminals. He walked with a straight-leg limp, having lost his entire knee joint in a horrific motorcycle accident while fleeing from police. He was a convicted felon, thus facing tremendous obstacles to employment and housing. His life was a mess, but while still living behind steel bars, Greg decided that, after his release, he was going to a place where he would be protected from the snares of the streets and where he could possibly find opportunities for a better future. His entire adult life had consisted of creating a mountain of destruction and debris, but the bones were good. There was life still inside him. There was hope and potential in spite of the mistakes of the past. There was a bright mind that was now fixed on the possibilities of the future and a chiseled will to take him there. Many questions remained unanswered, but the bones to build on were most definitely still good.

Over the past seventeen years, Greg Washington has committed himself daily to working and serving others. He began by volunteering and was given menial tasks, such as janitorial duties and organizing donations. He worked his way into a paid position with warehousing and custodial responsibilities but was a mainstay on the ministry teams that went out to feed the homeless, clean up the neighborhood, or otherwise bless the people in the community. After a few years of faithful service, Greg was elevated to Director of Youth Programming and returned to the streets where he once sold crack cocaine, but this time to pick up teenagers for after-school programs, ball games, retreats, and church services. In some instances, these kids were the children and grandchildren of people to whom he once sold drugs. Greg invested in them as if they were his own, deeply committed to offering them hope for a better life than the streets had to offer.

In my first book, *The Garden and the Ghetto*, which I wrote in 2010, there is a chapter called "Evolution," where I tell the story of Greg Washington up to that point. He had gone from being a good kid from a good family, to high school athlete and SeaWorld employee, to aspiring chef, to street thug and drug dealer, to a number in Georgia's prison system, to Youth Programming Director at City of Refuge. The "evolution" has continued. While still behind bars, Greg felt inspired that he would one day go back into the prisons, but this time through the front doors instead of the back gates. In 2019, Greg was tapped to lead a new initiative at COR—a prisoner re-entry program that would include teaching classes to men and women who were in their last twelve months of incarceration and implementing principles that would set them up for success upon release. The program also includes job training, family reunification, parenting and financial management classes, and mentoring.

Onto the good bones of the old Danzig Motel, City of Refuge has constructed The 345, a former eyesore that has become a showcase property in the community, with thirty-one efficiency apartments that are bright, fresh, and beautifully decorated. It will serve veterans, men who are re-entering society after release from prison, and young men from our community who are committed to furthering their education, are working full-time, or are enrolled in one of the City of Refuge vocational training programs.

Greg Washington was ragged and tattered when he walked through the gates in 2006, but onto the good bones that remained, he has built a life of purpose and productivity and works daily to teach and demonstrate to others that the same is possible for them. Every day he encounters men, whether in Georgia's prisons, or in the Workforce Innovation Hub, or elsewhere, who have whittled themselves down to nothing but bones, but those bones are good and the opportunity to add muscle is there. Greg mentors and counsels them, offers them opportunities for training and advancement, and perhaps most importantly, stands as an example of the good that can happen, even when there's nothing to work with but bones.

17

Lifers

In its simplest form, a life sentence
is the slow execution of a living being.
—SHANE BAUER

....

Every man dies. Not every man really lives.

WILLIE JACKSON and Bruce Hodge are boots-on-the-ground at The 345. Before the building was completed, Greg Washington had no doubt who the best guys to run the place would be. Just as he had turned the painful mistakes of his past into the pursuit of his purpose for the future, he knew these guys stood ready to use their experiences, both good and bad, to make a difference in the lives of the men they would serve in the newly formed program. Greg knew that the men who would walk those halls, sleep in those beds, and sit in those mentoring sessions would need to hear from guys who had already walked the pathway they were now on. He knew that books and journals would be important, lessons taught by knowledgeable people would provide information and inspiration, and programming and training would set them up for success and offset the distractions. But, most of

241

all, Greg knew that the men of The 345 would need to hear from other men who could truly identify with their situations. To a guy who just walked out of prison after being locked up for twenty years, the message that there is hope for a dynamic future, including a good paying job, affordable housing, and family reunification, would need to come from a living example and not just a teacher. Willie Jackson and Bruce Hodge are living examples.

BRUCE

At the sentencing hearing in the State of Georgia versus Bruce Hodge double murder trial in 1988, the judge spoke the following words: "I hereby sentence you to two consecutive life terms behind bars, plus one-hundred years. In other words, Mr. Hodge, the grandmother of any parole officer you may be dreaming of, has not yet been born." At eighteen years of age, Bruce Hodge did not fully comprehend the gravity of his situation. He was a child, albeit a child who had chosen a pathway usually reserved for malevolent adults, but a child, nonetheless. He had tried to prove himself a man by exacting force and control over other people, and he had lost any sense of the value of human life that may have been present in his childhood years. Physically, he could be counted as an adult male, but psychologically, his mind still functioned as a kid without the discretion and sound judgment that experience brings. This was illustrated by his decision to drop out of high school only weeks before the end of his senior year, and to dive into criminal activity as if there was a good future in it.

After hearing the judge's pronouncement, Bruce was escorted from the courtroom and taken back to the county jail. He felt numb and helpless but still maintained the attitude of a street survivor. After a few hours, he was transported to Alto State Prison in Alto, Georgia, where he would begin his "slow execution." He was in the company of a host of other very young inmates, and without older, seasoned prisoners to provide any sort of maturity or leadership, the atmosphere was one of chaos and violence. As Bruce puts it, "It was a free-for-all."

Life at Alto, which eventually became Lee Arrendale State Prison, was the epitome of survival-of-the-fittest. The young men were thrown into cell blocks together and left to fend for themselves. Bloodshed was a way of life and the absence of tranquility a given. There was no such thing as rational communication. The place was void of respect, either for the authorities or for fellow inmates, and every dispute was addressed at high volume and with the worst of language. Of course, fighting was almost always the ultimate resolution to conflict. Inmates from the central and southern regions of Georgia had taken offense to so many guys from the metro Atlanta area being sent to their facility, and a violent turf war had broken out. It was the stuff of prison movies.

After surviving a few years in the war zone at Alto, Bruce was transferred to Reidsville State Prison, a huge encampment affectionately known as "The Bottom," where he encountered an older and more sophisticated population, many of whom were also serving life sentences. It was still prison, the bars still cold and hard, the men still tough and committed to survival, but they were smarter in their approach and more calculating in their methods. Bruce, on the other hand, brought the wildness from Alto with him and continued to fight, gamble, and party like he did on the outside and at the more youthful facility. "I had not yet realized that I was locked up," he says. "I could do everything on the inside that I did on the outside, so I didn't really think about never getting out. I thought, *I can do this forever.*"

What Bruce didn't realize is that no long-term prisoner who makes it a habit to posture, threaten, fight, steal, and disrespect others ever lives to be an old man with stories to tell his children and grandchildren. They are found dead in their cells or are beaten until their brains are mush and they can never speak again. Sometimes the guards will turn their backs while it happens because they don't like the wild ones either. Bruce would need someone to give him a wake-up call, or his "slow execution" would be accelerated.

WILLIE

In the summer of 2018, Georgia's governor, Nathan Deal, opened Metro Reentry Facility as part of his criminal justice reform initiative. Metro first opened in 1980 as a men's prison, was converted to a women's facility in 1993, and was closed in 2011. After seven years of dormancy, it would now become a transitional center for male inmates in their last twelve months of incarceration. The initial roster of more than three hundred men was made up of those who had acknowledged the harm they had caused to society, had committed themselves to breaking cycles of crime, destruction, and poverty, and had shown aptitude and willingness to learn a new way of living. Included in the program were academic and vocational education opportunities, personal development, extracurricular activities, and community service, along with counseling and substance abuse recovery programming.

The governor and administrators from the Georgia Department of Corrections agreed that they would not hire professionals from the outside to teach the classes, run the programs, and mentor the inmates; rather, they chose twenty-five "lifers" from prisons around the state and transferred them to Metro to work with those who were preparing to re-enter society. These were men who had been incarcerated for many years for the violent crimes they had committed when they were young, and who had heard a judge tell them they would likely die in prison in a process of "slow execution." Among those lifers sent to Metro was Willie Jackson.

The decision to use lifers as leaders at Metro was brilliant. Although most of them were sure they would never live a moment outside prison walls, they had decided at some point to make the most of prison life and to take advantage of the opportunities that were offered. This was, after all, the life they were afforded, and the choice was theirs as to what they would make of it. Unknowingly, each of them had earned the right to be transferred from the usual state facilities, with large populations and all the typical prison problems, to the smaller and quieter Metro environment, where they would have the opportunity to invest in the lives of others. These were men who had risen to positions of peer leadership in Georgia's prison system and were viewed by wardens and other officials as stabilizers and father-figures. They had engaged in educational pursuits, both academic and vocational, had chosen to follow the rules and promote a clean and orderly atmosphere, and had led fellow inmates in spiritual pursuits. They were leaders in the prison programs and extracurriculars, and some of them had even started their own programs for the purpose of raising the quality of life for the population and giving opportunities for personal growth and development. Many of the men who benefitted from these offerings had never had the chance to participate in these kinds of things, even on the outside. As a matter of fact, many of them were there because of opportunity injustice.

In a story strikingly similar to that of Bruce Hodge, Willie Jackson was convicted of murder in 1989, and in January 1990 was sentenced to two consecutive life terms behind bars, plus forty years. He was twenty years old. Willie had given up on school after the eighth grade and had chosen a career on Atlanta's west side as a drug dealer, thief, and thug. His other felony convictions included armed robbery and aggravated assault.

On the day Willie Jackson was sentenced to life in prison, his girlfriend sat in the courtroom with their newborn baby in her arms. The judge asked Willie if he had anything to say before he was taken away, and Willie made a bold request. "Your honor," he said in a quavering voice, "would you allow me to hold my son before I go?" Surprisingly, the judge permitted Willie to sit in the jury box for fifteen minutes and hold his baby boy. Willie looked at the baby's face and saw himself and wondered if he would ever have a relationship with him. "I just have one request," Willie said to his girlfriend. "Just make sure my son knows who I am. Please, make sure he knows I'm his father."

The baby's name was Caderrian.

BRUCE

"I thought I would only leave prison toes-up," Bruce Hodge says as he reminisces on the hopelessness he felt when he started to realize he would probably be locked up for the rest of his life. The first five or six years had seemed more like a party in a different place, but now the years were stacking up and the losses were becoming more real. He had no education, poor communication skills, no vocational training or job experience, and the prospect of fighting his way through every life scenario started to seem pointless and fruitless, and he knew that one day he would lose the fight. Bruce had the sense that he was drowning in shallow water. Added to this recipe was the fact that older and wiser prisoners began to hold him accountable for his actions and to call his attention to the dead-end road he was choosing to travel. Guys with nicknames like Willie B. and Motorgrader said to him, "Look here, young buck, you're gonna be here. You can make it hard or you can make it easy, but you're gonna be here."

You're gonna be here. It settled in Bruce's spirit and things began to shift. He began to learn prison etiquette (yes, there is such a thing), and to give serious consideration to educational possibilities. He did a self-inventory and realized he had to start at ground zero and lay a foundation onto which he could build a productive life. If he was going to "be here," he decided he was going to "be here" as the best possible version of himself.

But the fallout of twenty-six years of reckless and irresponsible living did not vaporize because of a simple decision to do better. Bruce struggled with doubt, regret, guilt, and an array of other negative emotions. One night he sat alone in his cell, his cellmate having been transferred earlier that day. For the first time in his life, Bruce Hodge decided to give prayer a try; that is, at least prayer without an angle. He sat on his bunk and simply began a conversation with God, a conversation which began with the statement that he no longer wanted to live like he had been living. He poured out the frustrations, fears, and helplessness, and he asked God to take over. In Bruce's words, "In that moment, I broke. I wept to my core."

Behind Bruce Hodge was a war zone of destruction and chaos. He had grown up in the toughest neighborhood in the state of Georgia and had fallen into every trap that neighborhood had to offer young men like him. As a boy, he had very few positive influences and was starved of responsible, godly leadership. He turned to the streets and became a hardcore hustler and drug dealer. In 1989, two other dealers in the neighborhood attempted unsuccessfully to rob him. He could have chalked it up to the nature of the game. He could have simply claimed victory since they were unsuccessful, but in his world, reputation and status were everything, and he retaliated to preserve both. To send a loud and clear message, he killed the two men. He was arrested and charged with malice murder and felony murder, was found guilty by a jury of his peers, and was sentenced to two consecutive life sentences plus one hundred years by a judge who sent his own loud and clear message.

Now Bruce sat alone in a prison cell at three in the morning and started to release a well of anguish and sorrow onto the cell floor in a puddle of tears. He could have allowed the sorrow to form into more anger and become more bitter and violent than ever. He could have settled into a pit of hopelessness and found a way to take his own life. In order to protect his reputation and status, he could have sucked it up and continued to play the role of tough guy and survivor. Rather than choose any of the usual pathways, Bruce Hodge surrendered. He simply threw up his hands and told God he couldn't live this way anymore and that he was relinquishing control of his life and asking for help.

Make no mistake that Bruce's transformation was not instantaneous, but one good decision led to another until the good ones started to outnumber the bad. He knew what he wanted but was entirely clueless on how to get there. He started by working hard to obtain his GED. It was the first positive thing he had ever accomplished through hard work in his life, and it felt good. He enrolled in college courses and took every vocational class the prison had to offer. He gobbled up information like a hungry bear. "Kids simply act out what they've been told they are," Bruce says, but he decided to flip the script on the lying voices and prove them wrong.

Willie

Caderrian is thirty-two years old, and he sits by his father as if he is proud of the man. I suppose he should be. Willie Jackson was on the phone with his family the day Caderrian was born. Although locked away and awaiting trial prevented him from seeing or touching his newborn son, prohibited him from holding the one who would carry on his bloodline, he was determined to absorb as much of the experience as possible. Fortunately, the baby's mother was committed to making sure Caderrian knew who his father was and to facilitate as much of a relationship as was possible. Additionally, Willie's family was determined to keep him informed and involved with the most important things in his life, and Caderrian was at the top of that list.

Willie Jackson would spend three decades behind bars

for murder and aggravated assault. The early years were filled with anger, shock, denial, and grief, and when he was informed he was being sent to Reidsville State Prison, Willie was sure he was going there to die. At twenty years of age, he was thrown in with the general population. He had committed terrible crimes but was still a kid and was being thrown to the proverbial wolves. The birth of his son brought waves of regret from knowing he was not going to be there to see Caderrian grow up or to participate in his life. Although he cared deeply for her and desired a relationship with her, Willie told the child's mother to move on and find someone who could be a father-figure to Caderrian and provide a family structure for them. The young woman did just that, but she also honored Willie's request to keep his name and the reality of his existence in front of the child, and to make sure communication and visitation were regular parts of their lives.

Through the years, Willie Jackson has been the beneficiary of family support, and it has kept him alive and hopeful. The day he was sentenced to life in prison, his family was in the courtroom and their reaction was dramatic. He had made terrible mistakes and was going to pay the price for it, and they would pay as well, because the family always does. "But even if you don't have a family," Willie says, "create one. Find some good people and create one." That's the request he made of his girlfriend when he knew he would not be there to raise his son. *Find a good man, a man who will love, provide for, and protect my son from the traps that caught me. Find a good man who can build a family structure that Caderrian can grow up in. Make sure he knows who his father is, and that we have a relationship, but he will need someone that I can't be.*

BRUCE

"At some point, I had to evaluate the people in my life and decide what I wanted to be," Bruce says. "At some point, I had to evaluate my own biological father and make a decision about what kind of man I wanted to be. He came to visit me once while I was in prison. Pops, on the other hand, came to see me frequently."

"Pops" was the man Bruce's mother had married a short time after he went to prison. He had coached Bruce in football and had served as a guide to boys in the community, many of whom struggled with the vacuum created by the lack of strong and positive male leadership. Having turned the corner in his cell in a sort of Damascus Road moment, Bruce began to make decisions and take actions to break the cycles of crime and destruction in his own life and, hopefully, for others he would have the opportunity to influence. Like Willie, Bruce had a son on the way when he made the awful decision to commit violent crimes, but in his case, the child's mother did not keep the relationship alive and did not help to nurture a father-son relationship between Bruce and his child. From behind prison bars, Bruce had no control over the situation, and he has always grieved the loss, but he made the decision that he would invest in the lives of other young men, much like Pops did, even if the chance to have a relationship with his own boy was not there.

A decade is a long time, and many people who have been incarcerated for that long have given up hope and settled into a sad acceptance of their "slow execution." Bruce Hodge is the exception. After ten years in prison, he started to "turn selfishness into selflessness." With permission from prison officials, he started a support group called "Lifers," which was designed to offer guidance, mentorship, and practical support to inmates serving life sentences. Bruce encouraged mostly younger men to obey the rules, become leaders, take advantage of educational and training opportunities, and address the spiritual issues in their lives. In other words, he taught them to think and behave as if they would one day live again on the outside and could have a good life. Each of them had heard a judge say, "I sentence you to life in prison," but Bruce, once a dope dealer, became a hope dealer and encouraged his brothers that anything is possible and that they should make decisions that will make their life's journey positive and productive, no matter where that journey leads.

It didn't take long for Bruce to realize that one mentor was not enough to address the overwhelming needs among the population he was serving. In addition to the "Lifers" group, he initiated the "Lifers Mentors" group, which was designed to train other men to join the leadership team and become mentors as well. As time went on, and as guys were transferred to various facilities around the state, "Lifers" and

"Lifers Mentors" became life-changing entities in Georgia's prisons.

Through the years, Bruce had been called in for a handful of parole hearings, each time leaving the room with a rejection stamp on his paperwork, each time feeling dejected and more hopeless than ever. His expectation of leaving prison "toes-up" was validated by the parole board over and over. He remembered the judge's sarcastic declaration at his sentencing, that his parole officer's grandmother had not yet been born, and he accepted the process of "slow execution." However, Bruce's acceptance of his expected fate did not reduce him to a lump of clay that would simply waste away in a cell or die in a prison brawl. He had decided he would make the most of the life he had left and would spend his days making a positive difference in the lives of others. He was doing just that the day he was called in for his final parole hearing.

WILLIE

"God preserved me for something," Willie Jackson declares with a big smile on his face. Many times, while incarcerated, he had felt hopeless and that life behind bars was pointless. Like Bruce, Willie had sat before the parole board a few times and heard them say he had not yet paid his debt to society. The first hearing came at the seven-year mark, and he was excited to be able to inform members of the board that he was a different person and that he was ready to prove it. They smiled and nodded and told him they would see him again in another eight years. Their decision nearly sucked the life out of him, but he survived and sat before them again eight years later. Once again, they entertained his appeal that he was a changed man and acknowledged the efforts of family members to present themselves as a support system to Willie if he was released. The board members smiled, nodded, and told him they would see him again in another five years.

With the reality before him that he might never live a day outside prison walls, Willie had to decide: He could live selfishly, or he could live selflessly. He chose to turn the arrows outward and started to focus on ways he could make the situations of the guys around him better, ways that he could begin to perpetuate hope in the lives of mostly younger men who were void of strong male influences. If Willie could not have the life he wanted with his son, his mother, and other family members and friends, he would invest in his fellow inmates by proxy.

The support that came through the years from his family was monumental in Willie's life. He never felt abandoned, and although there were many days, weeks, months, and years of separation from the people he longed to be with, he never felt completely alone. Through visits, phone calls, letters, and financial support, his family members stuck by him and tried to make the best of the situation. His brother was among those who made sure Willie always had money on his books for things from the commissary that would make prison life a little more comfortable. Although there was no expectation that Willie should ever repay family members for their loving support, he struggled with a sense of obligation to do so. He often expressed to his brother that he wished there was some way to pay him back. Before his death in 2013, Willie's brother offered a pathway to clear the debt. "If you ever want to pay me back, just get out and do good." Willie knew the *getting out* part was a long shot, but he could *do good* no matter where he was. He would honor his brother's life and generosity by giving to others and enriching their lives. It was a pay-it-forward move that helped to break the chains of selfishness in his own life. The ripple effect would be colossal.

When Willie Jackson was informed that he was being transferred to Metro State Prison in Atlanta, he had no idea what the implications were. He knew he had been selected as one of the twenty-five "lifers" who would mentor inmates in their last twelve months of incarceration, and that he would have the opportunity to live out his days doing good works and inspiring men who would be given a second chance. In his mind, it was the best he could hope for. It was at Metro that Willie caught the attention of the warden and other leaders in the Department of Corrections. They witnessed his sincerity and the seriousness that went into his work with the guys in his charge. He was an innovator and a born leader. His humble charisma was received by the men he served as nothing but authentic and genuine. He cared about them and their futures. He was willing to give the rest of his life in service to others, and in doing so, would make his own life meaningful.

Warden Perkins started to believe in Willie more than ever. It was obvious the wild young criminal who had entered Georgia's penal system thirty years earlier had evolved into a mature and seasoned gentleman who had something positive to offer the world. The warden's recommendation to release Willie Jackson on parole was bittersweet; after all, Willie was the kind of inmate a warden longs for, one who brings calmness, hope, and positivity to the prison environment. But it was the right thing to do. Willie Jackson deserved the chance to live out his days with his family, the chance to spread his compassion and gifts in broader reaches, the chance for redemption.

"God preserved me for something," Willie declares. "He meant for me to go to Metro, and he meant for me to meet Greg Washington and to get involved in his program. With Greg, there was no judgment." He talks about how Greg validated him as a man and saw value in his life. Willie was in the very first cohort of TYRO, which was the initial name of the City of Refuge Re-entry and Reunification Program. He completed TYRO Dads, which focuses on father-child relationships and became a TYRO facilitator. It was another tool in his toolbelt to do the work he is convinced God has called him to do.

Willie's face forms into a smile of awe and disbelief when he describes getting the letter informing him that he would be transitioned to a half-way house where he would enjoy basic freedoms outside prison walls and would be allowed to start working and putting money away for the future. He was given a job at a chicken processing plant and saved $4500 in seven months. Although the idea seemed foreign, he was ready for his *future*. Thirty years earlier a judge had sentenced him to "slow execution" in the form of two life sentences plus forty years, and now, at fifty years of age, he was a free man. His full release came after seven months at the half-way house and Willie went to work at *DHL*. He fell in with his mother, brother, sister, aunts and uncles, and, of course, his son, Caderrian, as if he'd only been away on a long vacation. The cherry-on-top is that Caderrian has given Willie two beautiful grandchildren since he was released from prison.

BRUCE

You can't be serious, Bruce thought when he was interrupted in the middle of a Lifers mentoring session and told that the parole board was on site and wanted to see him. He had no time or patience for another meeting. He had zero interest in another formality highlighted by a foregone conclusion. He had important things to do. The guys in the room with him were now the focus of his efforts, and his goal was to lead them on the same pathway of transformation he had traveled. He no longer lived in a pipe dream that he would one day walk free.

Bruce asked the messenger to inform the parole board that he would like to be excused from the hearing because he was teaching a class and didn't have time for it. He didn't intend for his response to be dramatic and wasn't trying to produce shock waves among the board members, but it did just that. They were sure this man had lost his mind. After all, who turns down a parole hearing, even if the chances for a positive outcome are as slim as being bitten by a shark and struck by lightning in the same day. What they didn't know was that Bruce Hodge's turn from selfishness to selflessness was driving his entire existence. He was no longer focused on any good he may be able to realize for himself; rather, everything in his life was wrapped up in his efforts to help others.

In spite of his protests, Bruce Hodge was required to attend the hearing, and after serving twenty-four years of his sentence, was approved for parole.

Willie Jackson and Bruce Hodge are the beneficiaries of God's mercy and the *second chance* philosophy of City of Refuge. "We're living in a society that doesn't want to give second chances," Greg Washington says, "but City of Refuge believes in second chances." More than thirty years ago, two young men made egregious mistakes that resulted in monumental barriers to any possibility of a good, productive life. There is no attempt here to make excuses for their actions, and the resulting loss of life and the devastating impact that loss had on many people cannot be minimized. Both Willie and Bruce acknowledge what they did and live with a tremendous amount of remorse, but they have decided to make it part of their testimony and to use their mistakes to show others a

better pathway. Their decision to turn selfishness into selflessness is now breaking down barriers and building momentum
for others on a daily basis.

Willie Jackson left his job at DHL after three years
and was hired by Greg as a Residential Services Associate at
The 345. Today he invests in men who are returning from
incarceration, combat veterans dealing with PTSD or other
post-war issues, and young men from the neighborhood who
are looking for opportunities other than drugs and crime.
"I surrounded myself with people who were going the same
direction I wanted to go, and now we're going somewhere
good together."

When I ask Willie how he's getting along, he says, "I'm
thriving. My credit score is 767!"

Bruce Hodge served time with Greg at Hancock State
Prison but had no clue that many years later their paths
would cross again in a much different context. They now
work together as advocates and mentors through the City
of Refuge Re-entry and Reunification Program. Bruce is the
second-shift RSA at The 345. He sometimes looks from a
third-story window at the neighborhood where he grew up
and fell into a life of crime and violence, and wonders how
he got here. It's a full-circle experience, not unlike that of his
brothers Greg and Willie.

Unlike Willie, Bruce was not afforded the opportunity
to have a relationship with his son while he was in prison,
although he desired it deeply. Once he knew he was going

to be released, he hoped, albeit with reservations, that they could begin to build a father-son bond. However, in an almost unbelievable twist of irony, one week before Bruce's release, his son was sentenced to forty years in State Prison and was sent to the same facility, same dorm, and assigned the exact same cell as his father. Although the situation is heartbreaking, Bruce has his own story to offer hope to his son.

The "Lifers" are full of life and are relentlessly giving it away for the sake of others. Dry bones have come alive and are making a difference at The 345, in Atlanta, and in the world at large. These individuals once worked to see what they could get for themselves, and they came up empty. They now work to see what they can do for others, and in doing so have found exactly what they need.

18

Redemption Story: City of Refuge South

The moral arc of the universe is long, but it bends toward justice.
—MARTIN LUTHER KING, JR.

....

I HAD LET the people down, and for years I carried enough guilt to fill a tandem dump truck. Together we had a real shot at impacting our community in a positive way, making tangible and intangible differences through our good works, investing in kids and teens in a way that would make them better adults. But I had raised the white flag and walked away. I had bowed to the naysayers, traditionalists, and bigots and told them they could have it to do as they pleased. The guilt was enormous. It affected my ability to be good at the next thing I chose to do. It affected my marriage and my performance as a father. It even affected my health. Stress settled in my lower back, and frequent spasms were the result. I experienced headaches and fatigue. I was often moody and would have likely been diagnosed with the "D" word if I had given a mental health professional the opportunity to pronounce it. I'm glad I didn't. I may have embraced it as part of my identity.

After my departure, it would be five years before I started working with Bruce, but even after teaming up with him, I dealt with the guilt for another five.

The year was 1989, and I had finally succumbed to an internal compulsion to enter the ministry. I had put out a fleece, as they say, and announced that I would have to be unemployed, broke, and homeless before I would follow in the footsteps of my father and brother and announce my candidacy for church work. Five months after my statement of defiance, I had lost my job, could not pay the rent, and was moving my family in with my wife's mother. If I had been single, I would have moved to a shack in the woods and lived on squirrels and berries, but I had mouths to feed, as they say, and those mouths were not too keen on squirrel.

Okay, I hear ya, I thought, *maybe we can figure something out on this ministry thing.*

I decided to take a shot at being a youth pastor; after all, getting paid to hang out with teenagers—going bowling, eating pizza, playing Bible trivia, and sitting in a circle singing "It only takes a spark . . ." didn't seem so bad. I sent out my résumé, and it proved good enough to get me an interview for a part-time position at a church in Thomaston, Georgia. The pastor was a long-time friend of my parents, so he was willing to overlook my inexperience, lack of training, and shoddy work history.

I went for the interview and learned that the church had about fifteen active teens and that they could not afford to pay a full-time salary, but if I would agree to come, they could pay me a part-time salary and I could work at the Piggly Wiggly supermarket that was managed by a church member. I accepted the offer, but by the time we arrived in Thomaston three weeks later, the manager at Piggly Wiggly had been fired and there was no job. I began looking for other opportunities but was unsuccessful.

In terms of active membership, programs, and activities, the church was thriving with a Sunday morning attendance of four hundred. There was a heavy emphasis on music, especially choirs and "special" music, which I sometimes thought was not so special at all. The church was known for its music productions and plays, especially at Easter and Christmas. They were strong on programming for children, but the weak spot in the whole business was with the youth. The previous part-time youth pastor had left for greener pastures; thus, the decision was made to bring in a Dream Team of one—me— with no experience other than the fact that I had grown up in church, which had mostly taught me the wrong way to deal with teenagers. The cherry-on-top was the $800 per month salary with no benefits.

We initially moved in with the pastor and his wife, which prompted him to work harder to find another source of income for me. The church had a part-time secretary who wanted to quit but who had agreed to stay on until they could find a replacement. One day, the pastor timidly asked if I'd like to take on the secretarial responsibilities, thus creating a situation where I could be full-time at the church. I agreed to answer the phone, sort the mail, produce a weekly bulletin, and make copies, but made sure he knew my dictation and typing skills were deficient.

Tracy and I made immediate connections with the teens and quickly embraced the opportunity to do life with them and to offer whatever spiritual or practical guidance we had to give. Just days before our arrival, the church and youth group had been rocked by the death of the fourteen-year-old son of a prominent church family. He and his older brother were struck by a drunk driver who ran a stop sign, and the brother, Chris, was still in critical condition in a hospital in Columbus. The situation had caused the core group of young people to band together and draw closer to one another and to support Chris and his family. In their vulnerability and grief, we were able to minister to them and pray for them in ways that knitted us together for life. More than thirty years later, many of them are still our good friends.

Our numbers began to grow, and within a few months, I was relieved of the secretary job in order to work full-time with a group that by now was nearly thirty students. We played ball, had "afterglows" at different homes on Sunday nights, went on retreats, studied and prayed together, had lock-ins in the gym, and to satisfy the desires of the almighty music program, formed a youth choir. Things were going well.

Then came the big shift.

Bruce was back in Virginia and was serving as Youth Pastor at the home church of many of our relatives. He had a thriving group and had decided to stretch them by experimenting with urban missions. He contacted a small church in the inner city of Charleston, West Virginia, found out their building needed a roof replacement and that they were located in a neighborhood consisting of housing projects and poverty-stricken residents. Plans were made to take his group to Charleston for a week of working on the building and conducting outreach efforts to kids in a neighboring park. His team would sleep in the church basement and take their meals in the sanctuary. For a group of kids from the equivalent of Mayberry, USA, it was as raw and risky as it gets.

Then came the call from Bruce to me that went something like this: "How would you like to bring some of your kids to West Virginia to spend a week ministering to people?"

"Huh?"

"Yeah, it'll be fun. It'll expose them to things they've never seen. It might cause some of them to get more serious about their faith and stir them up about serving others."

"Huh?"

"Let's do it. We'll plan a combined mission trip and it'll be awesome."

"Okay."

"Awesome" fails miserably in its attempt to describe the experience we had in Charleston. I pressed through the resistance I faced from my pastor and the church board and took a dozen kids on the trip, and it changed our lives. Our purpose in going was to positively impact a small, struggling church and the neighborhood that surrounded it, and we accomplished that mission, but the impact it also had on our group, beginning with me, was immeasurable. Out of that week, we began to conduct an annual youth retreat called Jesus Jam that impacted thousands of teens and youth leaders for the next twenty-five years. Most importantly, out of that week, many of us had to deal with a fire that had been kindled in our hearts, a fire that would lead us into the impoverished and underprivileged neighborhoods in our own towns, a fire that would not let us rest until we had crawled into the ditch with the poor and offered ourselves as a resource to facilitate a knowledge of God and a better life.

When we arrived back in Thomaston, the transformation that was taking place in our group was palpable. The kids were more serious in their worship and prayer. They had a greater hunger for Truth and were much more engaged in the processes of spiritual growth. Most of all, they were champing at the bit to get out into the community and serve the population. We began to do "Sidewalk Sunday School" on Saturday mornings in a couple of government housing complexes. I had read a book called *Whose Child is This?* by Bill Wilson, the founder and director of Metro Ministries in New York City. His team was reaching thousands of children weekly with their "Sidewalk Sunday School" program. I decided to scale the model to our small town, and we started showing up weekly in the neighborhoods.

Initially, we were greeted with an attitude of reservation that bordered on suspicion. The people who lived in those neighborhoods were not accustomed to visitors from the outside unless the cops were serving a warrant or an insurance salesman was peddling a product. Little by little, they warmed up to us as they realized we were there to bless the kids and their families and wanted nothing in return. We learned their names, fed them snacks, gave away prizes, entertained them with puppets and music, and finished up with a short devotion and prayer.

Then came the question, "Can I come to your church on Sunday?" It came from a boy or girl, I don't remember which, but it opened the door for an avalanche of similar questions and comments.

"Yeah, can I come too? I wanna come."

"Me too. If he gets to come, so do I, right?"

I decided to use Wednesday nights as our testing ground, and the first Wednesday we picked up four kids in my minivan. Over the next few weeks, we filled up my van and the church's fifteen-passenger van. Tracy and I, our youth leadership team, and a significant number of the teens in the youth group were doing the work—providing transportation, preparing food, conducting the programming, maintaining crowd control, etc. We soon had a couple dozen kids coming on a regular basis.

Then it started. The old man stopped me in the hallway on a Sunday morning between the Sunday school hour and morning worship. "Hey, Deel," he growled, "why are you bringing those n——s to our church?"

"I'm sorry, what?" I replied, sure I had not actually heard what I thought I heard from this elder, this long-time church member, this tithe-payer, this advisor to the pastor, this "Christian."

"Yeah, you pass two n—— churches between here and over where they come from. You need to stop and drop them off. We don't want them here." He walked away with a snort and a sneer.

I felt like I had been punched in the gut and wanted to throw up. I had been raised in the South and was aware that racist attitudes were still prevalent, even in the church, but these were kids, not some lower form of animal that needed to be shooed off to a location that was more suited for their kind. The idea of being in a place that exists for the purpose of worshiping God, who is the personification of love, grace, and mercy, and to witness hatred, intolerance, and harsh judgment toward innocent children, especially from a leader among the people, presented one of the greatest and most tragic ironies I've ever witnessed. I was angry and wanted to unleash a barrage of retaliatory words. I was frustrated to know that a supposed believer and church member would not support efforts to lead children from our community in a positive direction. But, most of all, I was very sad.

I waited until Monday morning to share the experience with the pastor and expected him to be as shaken as I was. He wasn't. He immediately expressed that he was aware that there was a rumbling in the congregation about what we were doing. "Not everybody, mind you, but some are not happy." He rambled about how he loved and supported the outreach, and was even "okay" with us bringing kids to church, but we needed to scale back the number. We needed to be more "inconspicuous" about it. He laced his commentary with side notes that let me know he liked me and wanted to support my efforts, but that he also had board members and tithe payers to "keep happy." Ultimately, he made sure I understood that it wasn't my job that was on the line, but his.

The following week, I received resignations from two long-time volunteers in the kids' department. Each of them offered the same reason—"We will serve our own, but not them." More rumbling. I scaled back the numbers as the pastor had instructed but felt disingenuous when offering excuses to the kids about why they could no longer come. I certainly wasn't going to tell them the truth: that God-fearing church members hated them because they were black. The rumbling grew louder until the pastor decided it was time to look for greener pastures. He swapped churches with a man from South Georgia, and it may have solved his dilemma, but it certainly didn't solve ours.

The new pastor heard the rumbling before he finished unloading his U-Haul truck and came through the door on a mission to get rid of me. I only wish he had simply told me to get out and never come back. After all, he was the boss and had the authority to do so. Instead, he complimented me, hugged my neck, and told me how proud he was to serve alongside me, and left unexpected bonus checks on my desk, all the while slicing me up like Jack the Ripper behind my back. Six months into his tenure, I raised the white flag.

By this time, Bruce had moved to Atlanta and was working at the suburban church that eventually sent him to Midtown Mission, which became City of Refuge. His pastor and boss, Darrell Rice, offered me a position as Director of Family Ministries, and I accepted. During our time there, Tracy and I were blessed to travel to Jamaica as part of short-term missionary teams and were eventually asked to move to the island to live and work full-time.

Now, moving a family that includes a wife who is very close to her mother, as well as four children between the ages of ten and two, to another country is a pretty big deal. Tracy relished the experiences we had in Jamaica but was nervous and hesitant about such a big move, especially with four young children as part of the equation. We took some time to talk, pray, and consult with others about the situation. I was sure the work would be fulfilling and productive. I had been asked to develop a basic academic program at the Institute of Caribbean Missions, a Christian vocational training center for young men. They offered training in welding, carpentry, and horticulture but were facing challenges with students who couldn't read or write. Additionally, I was excited about the possibility of living in another country and exposing our children to Jamaican culture. But we needed confirmation.

"Well, I think God has given me a sign that we should go," Tracy said as I arrived home from work one afternoon. She told me to get back in the car. We drove a mile down the road, and she pointed to a brand-new billboard for an airline we'd never heard of—Air Jamaica. The caption read, "Come to Jamaica and feel alright!"

A literal sign.

Our time in Jamaica was most certainly fulfilling and productive, but I still carried the guilt of my decision to leave Thomaston. Tracy carried it as well. Perhaps I would have been fired anyway. Perhaps I quit because I knew the firing was inevitable and this was my way of controlling the situation and preserving my pride. Perhaps there was no chance of succeeding in such a toxic environment, and that I was living in a pipe dream to think we could redirect the hearts and souls of a church and community. In any case, guilt was prevalent and it affected our lives tremendously.

We had let the kids in the neighborhood down and couldn't help but wonder if our departure would result in the loss of opportunity to know God and follow his ways. We had abandoned the teens in our youth group and figured there was little possibility that they would continue to grow in their faith and do good works without proper leadership. We loved the town and wanted to invest in it, especially in the youth and kids, and although we left them, they never left our hearts or prayers.

When we returned from Jamaica and I started to work with Bruce, we settled in Pike County, only fifteen miles north of Thomaston. Tracy's mother had retired there and was alone. We put a little house on land that she gifted to us and decided we would raise our children in the country the way I grew up. For twenty-four years, I commuted sixty miles each way to City of Refuge, and for many of those years, we went to the city on Sundays as well to attend church at The Mission, but Thomaston still held a place in our hearts. We were frequently in the town as it was home to the nearest grocery stores, restaurants, banks, and other businesses and conveniences. Sometimes, Tracy and I would pull into the church parking lot and say a prayer that God's kingdom would come and his will would be done in that place. We heard rumors that things were not good with the church and that attendance had dwindled to a few mostly elderly people. Once or twice, we happened to be in Thomaston on a Sunday morning at the eleven o'clock hour and saw only a dozen or so cars in the parking lot. We prayed that the right thing would happen for the church and the community.

Around 2008, we finally pulled the lever on the dump truck bed and unloaded the guilt. I was experiencing a level of burnout from the mental and emotional drain of working daily with people in the city, people who were living in the throes of brokenness and who leaned heavily on us to help them find healing and restoration, to provide answers to their questions, to resolve their confusion. Additionally, we had five children at home between the ages of sixteen and six, and I was driving a hundred and twenty miles a day back and forth to work. Following the advice of my wife, I went away for a mini retreat and returned with renewed energy and commitment. One of the things I came to understand was that I was making my situation much worse by choosing to carry a heavy sack of guilt on my shoulders at all times. That's right, it was a choice, and now I made the choice to let it go. I wanted to be the best husband, father, minister, and employee that I could possibly be, and guilt was simply not part of the recipe.

Four years later, friends we had known from Thomaston since our days of working at the church in the early nineties asked if we would help them organize some community outreach efforts in their town. They knew about our work in Atlanta and had a desire to do good works among their own population but didn't know how. Although our lives were already busy and demanding, we said yes and started to talk through ideas. We organized a Friday night support group for anyone who was struggling with issues and needing encouragement, prayer, instruction, and counsel. We rented a small house and filled it up with people who were battling addictions to drugs, alcohol, and pornography, as well as people who were dealing with extreme grief, fear, depression, oppression, and anxiety. We outgrew the house and moved into a warehouse space in the back of a friend's business.

For the next four years, we met weekly to eat food, share in worship and fellowship, and bear one another's burdens. We placed individuals into addiction recovery programs and walked the journey to freedom with them. We wrapped our arms around those who had suffered loss and did our best to fill the gaps. We conducted Matthew Parties in impoverished neighborhoods, which involved cooking food and inviting the community to come eat with us, giving away household goods such as mattresses, towels, socks, light bulbs, and potted flowers. We played games with the kids and visited with the adults. We made ourselves available for spiritual counsel and prayer, but in a non-threatening way. In other words, we did what we had wanted to do twenty-nine years earlier.

In January 2017, on a whim, I said to Bruce, "Hey, why don't you reach out to the denomination chief and ask him what's happening with the church in Thomaston." I had heard that the pastor was planning to retire, and that they could not find anyone who was willing to take the church. Bruce made the call and a meeting was set for early February.

We sat in Bruce's conference room and learned that the church was dying, literally, with a handful of brethren left, and an average age in the seventies. According to Administrative Bishop Tom Madden, they were three to five years from padlocking the doors and selling the property. He was sched-uled to meet with the members the following Wednesday night but did not know what to tell them. All he knew was that he was heartbroken that this beautiful facility, with a sanctuary that would seat five hundred, tons of classroom space, a magnificent gymnasium, and full commercial kitchen, located in a prime location on the main thoroughfare, was serving only as a museum that housed relics from its glory days.

We told him we had a solution and asked him to inform the members that he was turning the church and property over to City of Refuge, and that we would be bringing our already vibrant ministry into the facilities, and that any of them who wanted to stay and join us were welcome.

And that's exactly what he did.

Two months later, we moved in and City of Refuge South was born. Today we operate a dynamic program for kids from the community, with dozens of them receiving the benefits of tutoring and mentoring during the school year. During the summer they spend a week at Camp Lighthouse in the North Georgia mountains, go fishing at the South Pond, go for peach ice cream at Dickey's Farm, and swim in any pool that's offered. They participate in a fantastic Vacation Bible School and learn about life in relationship with God through Kids Church and devotional times. This summer we even took a few of them to Jamaica and gave them the experience of serving others in a foreign land.

We continue to refer people to recovery programs and to provide supplemental support. We conduct huge food distributions twice a month, with as many as a hundred and fifty cars coming through and picking up food at each distribution. We provide practical assistance to needy families and have facilitated entry to House of Cherith for a few ladies from our area.

In other words, we are doing everything we wanted to do thirty years ago, and then some!

Early in 2019, my son, Sully, took interest in a beautiful ninety-acre tract of land that borders the church property. I told him to track down the owner and find out what the intention was for the parcel. The owner did not have the land for sale but said he had held onto it until its "highest and best use" became apparent. Our reply was, "Well, here we are."

In November of that year, we acquired the property by donation for the purpose of creating a therapeutic recreational facility, including an equestrian center with a modest barn, round pens, covered arena, and riding trails, as well as a multi-purpose play field, basketball and volleyball courts, archery range, climbing wall, zipline, pool, and a small chapel.

Because of the pandemic and other factors, our plans for the land have been slow coming together, but in spring of 2023, we broke ground and launched into phase one of the project. Presently, engineers are doing the preliminary work so that things can be designed properly and placed rightly on the land. We look forward to serving kids, veterans, groups from the different House of Cherith locations, local sports teams, law enforcement and fire and rescue personnel, and many others.

It's a redemption story that cannot be explained or understood outside of Providence. It's God, in response to obedience, taking what's wrong and making it right. To him be the glory.

RISK

Like the leper at the city gate I sit at the base of this mountain
And all the world lies behind it
Perhaps a canyon of colors, the gold aspens of autumn,
a meadow in flowers or snow
Or perhaps the next mountain,
with a peak that summons

Mother arrives with counsel—
wear your helmet and keep it tight,
take care lest you get caught in a storm,
don't talk to strangers
And Mother bears a treasure trove of wisdom
and is right when she points out that the wind forms
a jet stream through that cut in the rock
Ignoring the risk will unhinge you, like a particle in space

But, like the leper, if I sit here, I die
And if I choose to climb, perhaps I die
Yes, perhaps I die, but at least I die knowing
For on the other side of that mountain is all the glory
And all the tragedy
And both enrich the soul

—JEFF DEEL

19

Communities: An Epidemic of Good Works

No space of regret can make amends
for one life's opportunity misused.
—Charles Dickens

....

City of Refuge has targeted the 30314 and 30318 zip codes in Atlanta, Georgia, for more than twenty-five years. As described earlier, by virtue of my status with the parent organization, as well as my relationship to Bruce, City of Refuge South was an organic offshoot that developed when I started doing outreach in the small town near my home. As well, after we left Jamaica in 1998, we continued to travel there and to work among the poor and support small churches in mountain communities. It, too, became an offshoot that we named Refuge Jamaica. "Jamerican, that's what you are, a Jamerican," is what one precious old Jamaican lady labeled me early on. It seems I have Jamaica in my blood and can't get rid of it. Through the years I have led hundreds of short-term missionaries to the island to do City of Refuge-style ministry. We have built churches from the ground up, put on numerous roofs, added space to small buildings, laid tile, painted walls, installed bathrooms, office space, and baptistries, run wiring and plumbing, and just about anything else involved in construction. Last summer we built a house from the ground up for a grandfather who is raising his four grandchildren, and we funded construction of another house for a single dad whose wife was murdered.

With a big emphasis on education, we have painted, remodeled, and built additions onto school buildings and provided truckloads of school supplies and educational materials. One of the most fulfilling aspects of Refuge Jamaica ministries is the monthly sponsorship of school children, with stipends to cover fees, supplies, uniforms, lunch money, and bus fare. We leave them without an excuse to not stay in school. At any point in time there have been up to fifteen children receiving this support on a monthly basis. Twenty-five years in, we now have a few kids whose sponsorships started when they entered kindergarten and continued until they graduated high school. One, Reniel, obtained a degree from University of the West Indies and is studying to be a veterinarian. Refuge Jamaica supported him through a sixteen-year educational journey.

Additionally, we have been blessed to sponsor many adults and children with disabilities and to assist senior adults with money for food and prescription medications. This is a vital ministry on the island, and it continues today.

Like a train starting with a slow chug but gaining momentum little by little, the move toward establishing City of Refuge campuses and operations in other towns and cities has been ramping up for the past few years. Including Atlanta and South, there are now five City of Refuge organizations in Georgia. Tim and Sharon Langston were part of Midtown Mission church for nearly twenty years when they started City of Refuge in their hometown of Calhoun. They have a local church, conduct a variety of outreach programs in the community, and run a dynamic Celebrate Recovery program for recovering addicts.

Geoff and Connie Rushing got their start in benevolent work by taking teams from their church to Jamaica to be part of what Refuge Jamaica was doing. For a dozen years they have been involved in our work on the island, but two years ago, an inner fire started for them to do something in their own community. City of Refuge Athens has grown to be a force in Clarke and Oconee Counties, with food, school uniforms and supplies, and other resources going out to hundreds of children and their families. They recently launched an after-school tutoring and mentoring program that is gaining traction by the minute. Early on, they asked me if I had any advice as they prepared to respond to the call.

"Fasten your seatbelts," I said. "If you say yes to this, it's going to be an adventurous journey." They frequently remind me that it was good advice.

The great state of Virginia is also home to three City of Refuge campuses. In 2006, Joe and Kelly Blankenship founded The Rock Youth Center in Pulaski to address the needs of wayward high schoolers in their county. They had served in traditional youth ministry but felt the kids in the community would respond better to a nontraditional approach. Sixteen years later, they are City of Refuge Pulaski and continue to work with the youth and provide health and wellness programs and job training.

Thurman and Vickie Collier moved to Hopewell in 2007 to serve as pastor of a local church. They are still pastoring the church but also run a residential drug recovery program, job placement services, and high-quality early childhood education. City of Refuge Hopewell opened in 2018 and is a lighthouse in their community.

Chafik Laaissaoui, a former Muslim from Morocco, along with his wife, Ella, pastor a local church in South Hill and became a City of Refuge community in 2017. They have a heavy emphasis on education and outreach to youth and kids, as well as food distribution and practical assistance to needy families.

Baltimore is one of the most crime infested and violent cities in America, but City of Refuge Baltimore is shining Light, perpetuating Hope, and facilitating Transformation. Under the leadership of Billy and Sarah Humphrey, it is the most similar to the Atlanta operation, with an active Health and Wellness program, job training, supportive housing, programming for youth and kids, and a recently launched House of Cherith for women rescued from trafficking. So far this year, they have placed sixty-one people in full-time jobs and have assisted eight veterans in starting their own businesses.

Under the leadership of Stephanie Marquardt, City of Refuge Chicago focuses on providing solid, safe sports programs for kids, working with local police in maintaining high quality leagues, while establishing strong, trusting relationships between law enforcement and young citizens. They also operate a Resource Center, providing counseling, financial literacy classes, and assistance with groceries and household goods.

The future of many neighborhoods across the nation is bright as plans come together for the establishment of City of Refuge operations. With the support and endorsement of many influential persons and entities, as well as the commitment of significant financial backing, plans are underway for the launch of City of Refuge Nashville in the near future. It, like Baltimore, will include nearly all the same programs and services as the mother ship. Early next year will also see the official beginning of City of Refuge in the Atlanta suburb of East Point. As well, conversations are underway around potential sites in Las Vegas, Tampa, St. Charles, Missouri, and Lancaster, Ohio.

As I said in chapter 1, the work of City of Refuge often carries with it the import of life or death. Even in our attempts to provide a lifeline to anyone who comes our way, we have lost many—Michael, Kenny, Dennis, Gloria, Ken, Deb, Sarah, Whoopie, Brittney, Jonathan, and Jennifer—to name a few. Each of these lives was valuable, regardless of the depressing details of their stories and their demise. Each of them gave us their love to the extent they knew how, and each of them received our love, best intentions, and effort. All of the City of Refuge entities above are finding it necessary to chart their losses as well, as does every church, ministry, nonprofit, recovery program, and human services organization on earth. It's part of living in a broken world.

But it's the lives that are saved that keep us going. It's the playing out of the Light, Hope, and Transformation process that results in beautiful, powerful testimonies of healing, freedom from addiction, freedom from the rule of pimps and taskmasters, financial stability, restored family relationships, expunged criminal records, career pathways, and even home ownership.

It is Rufus who keeps us going, who after twenty years of homelessness, addiction, and hustling on the streets, for more than a decade has been clean and sober, maintaining his own residence, and living a lifestyle of worship to God and service to his fellow man. It is Greg who inspires us to get up and do Good Works again today. He moved from crack cocaine dealer on Atlanta's streets, to long-term resident in Georgia's penal system, to janitor at City of Refuge, to Level-Up Youth Director and Youth Pastor at The Mission, to a member of the Executive Team as the Director of Re-entry. He now spends the hours of his days facilitating Light, Hope, and Transformation for men and women who are where he once was.

It is Holly and Katherine who motivate us to receive the next girl in crisis with open arms and a commitment to being the family she desperately needs. They are models of obedience to the process and have both made tremendous progress in their journey to restoration and wholeness. In addition, they now serve on the City of Refuge team and invest daily in the lives of women and children who are still in the program

Rufus, Greg, Holly, and Katherine are representative of thousands who have entered the gates broken but found their pathway to healing. City of Refuge Communities are causing those numbers to explode around the country, and each number is a life, and each life is valuable and significant. The addict in Hopewell is finding his family and freedom. In Baltimore, the single mom, who was a victim of domestic violence, is discovering genuine love and enjoying her new apartment. The homeless poor in Nashville don't know what's coming, but it's going to be good.

20

No End in Sight

Into the great wide open, under the skies of blue.
Out in the great wide open, a rebel without a clue.
—TOM PETTY

....

BRUCE IS UNSETTLED. He will be sixty-three years old in a few days and there is no sign of slowing down, no talk of retirement, no fading off into the sunset. As I stated in a previous chapter, he frequently declares that we will do more in the next five years than we have done in the previous twenty-five. I'm starting to think he is serious. I'm starting to believe it will happen.

Recently, Bruce has become impassioned about challenging other men to get involved in the fight against sex trafficking. "Men are the problem," he declares, emphatically, "and men must be the solution." There are no excuses. In addition to MOST (Men Opposing Sex Trafficking), he launched BEST (Boys Eliminating Sex Trafficking). The time has come to teach boys to respect the royalty of their mothers, sisters, and female friends. It's time to turn the tide of destructive ideologies that are poisoning our children from the inside out. It's time for a reversal of the sexualization of our culture. It's time for young boys to hear the truth about the dangers of pornography. Bruce is rallying an army of men and boys to take a stand against the fastest growing criminal enterprise in the world by identifying traffickers and working with law enforcement to bring them to justice, rescuing survivors, and creating environments for hope and healing.

One block from the City of Refuge campus, we are preparing to break ground on a new Transformation Center. The beautiful three-story center will feature a medical and mental health clinic for survivors of trafficking and domestic violence, a social entrepreneurship hub, a healthcare call center, and the first credit union opened in the state of Georgia in thirty years. The upper floors will also contain several affordable living spaces.

The Transformation Center will expand our ability to fill the gaps in economic, health, and wellness services on Atlanta's west side, as well as adding much needed housing options.

To further enhance affordable housing possibilities on Atlanta's west side, plans are in place for construction of the Andrews Street Townhomes on the hill above the City of Refuge campus. Sixteen families will have the chance to live in beautiful new permanent supportive housing units, with a ten-year ownership plan for the residents to purchase the homes at zero percent interest. Sixteen families will have the opportunity to move from homelessness to transitional living, to supportive housing, to first-time home ownership. Now that's Transformation.

With these plans in place, as well as increased support for City of Refuge Communities around the country and planned improvements to the Atlanta campus, there is no end in sight. Bruce's answer to the retirement question is, "I want to work until I'm ninety, then get hit by a truck."

My plan is to continue to follow the leader. As long as my wagon is hitched to his star, we will end up in the same place. I will only stop following when it's my time to depart this earth. Rather than making my exit on the bumper of a Peterbilt, I think I'll just pass peacefully in my sleep. Either way, it is well with our souls.

....

A Letter to
Cecil and Dawn

DEAR DAD AND MOM,

Since the separate glorious spring days in May 2017 and
2019, when we laid your bodies to rest on a peaceful hillside
in Dublin, Virginia, I have not visited your graves. Some folks
frequent the cemeteries where their loved ones are buried, I
suppose to make sure the plot is properly maintained and the
flowers are fresh and seasonal, or perhaps to chat for a while
because the painful thought of losing the monumentally
important element of human communication is more than
they can bear. Others may do so because something in life
was left undone and they are hoping to bring it to completion, at least in their own hearts.

I understand all of this, I think. Once, on a visit to
California, Tracy and I went to a cemetery where many
famous people are buried. When we drove onto the property, we were surprised to see the landscape dotted with lawn
chairs, blankets, and picnic baskets, much like you would see

at the park. People were making a day of sitting by the plots of their loved ones, choosing to keep company with the dead over all other possibilities.

I don't question or judge any of this. When a person leaves this world, those left behind must deal with it in whatever manner works for them. I have experienced two emotional earthquakes in my life—they happened on the days each of you left—and they taught me that there is no way to plan for the tsunami of grief that will follow. You may think you're ready, but you're not. Although no method can completely fill the void that is created by such monumental loss, or can cause the pain to ultimately disappear, I have discovered the method of navigating life without you that works best for me, and I respect the methods of others.

Not only have I not visited your graves, but I don't talk about you very much. The memories are there. The stories never fade. The emotions are as deep as they've ever been. No son has ever honored his parents more than I honor you, and no recipient of pristine heritage has been more grateful. It's just that the mention of your names causes my heart to crack a little more and my voice to quaver like a child in trouble. In his memoir *Ava's Man*, Rick Bragg, when speaking of the death of the family matriarch, writes, "An odd thing happened. The children stopped talking about her very much because it hurt them so bad to touch her in their memories, and what good is that?"[1]

---

1 Rick Bragg, *Ava's Man* (New York: Vintage, 2002).

That's how I feel.

I have a feeling my children discuss it behind my back, how I don't talk about you, or tell all the stories I told when you were alive, or reminisce about times and situations in which you were the central figures. I don't try to explain it, because to try to explain it would be as painful as touching you in my memory by telling a story. So, I just keep my mouth shut. They probably figure that one day the shackles will drop off and I will find my freedom. Maybe.

If an apology for not visiting your graves is appropriate, I offer it here, but, somehow, I reckon in my spirit that your feelings are not hurt. One day I may bring a lawn chair and a sandwich to Highland Gardens and hang out for a while, but that'll be when I'm too old and weak to do anything else. In the meantime, I think I'll continue to do what you taught me to do—to provide a sandwich and a comfortable spot to some weary soul on whom the cares of life have trampled. I think I'll keep following your model of loving and taking care of widows and orphans and of trying to help captives find a pathway to freedom. I think I will love, give, forgive, and extend the benevolent heart of God to a troubled world, because that's what you did, and it's what the world needs.

And it's not just me. I have followed your oldest son my entire life, and I will continue to follow him on his quest to provide Light, Hope, and Transformation. It may seem odd, but his quest has become my own. Keith and April, the younger (and definitely more spoiled) favorites, carry the torch of their heritage as well, living and moving and having their being in the Spirit you introduced them to. Most of your grandchildren fully embrace the legacy of grace and good works that trickled down from your lives, and the rest will get there one day.

I have a sneaking suspicion that you will give me a pass on the cemetery visitation.

I love you,

Jeff

Acknowledgments

....

To MY WIFE, Tracy, and our lovely passel of children, who have always encouraged me to cultivate my gifts, and have given me room to do so. I love you all.

To MY BROTHER, Bruce, whom I have followed through flood and fire, across mountain and valley, and from the country to the city. He gave me a story to write.

To THE GREATER City of Refuge family, including loyal co-laborers and the people we serve. You are the heroes; we're just the guides.